FOR ORGANS, PIANOS & ELECTRONIC KEYBOARDS

145

ISBN 978-1-4234-9626-7

HAL•LEONARD®
CORPORATION

7777 W. BLUEMOUND RD. P.O. BOX 13819 MILWAUKEE, WI 53213

Visit Hal Leonard Online at
www.halleonard.com

Bless His Holy Name

Registration 2
Rhythm: March

Words and Music by
Andraé Crouch

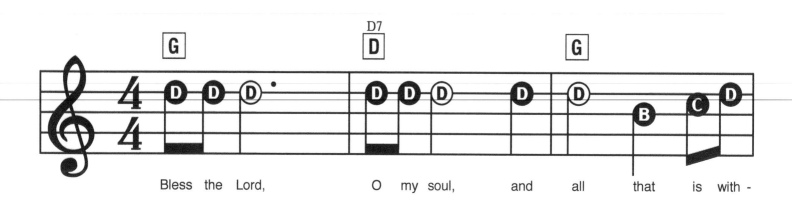

Bless the Lord,   O my soul,   and   all   that   is   with -

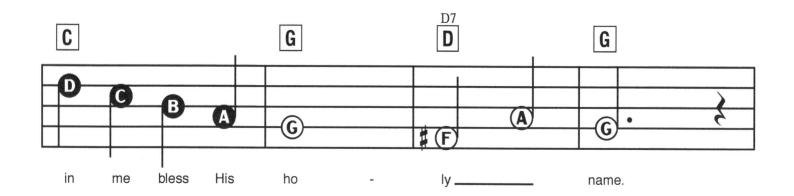

in   me   bless   His   ho   -   ly _____   name.

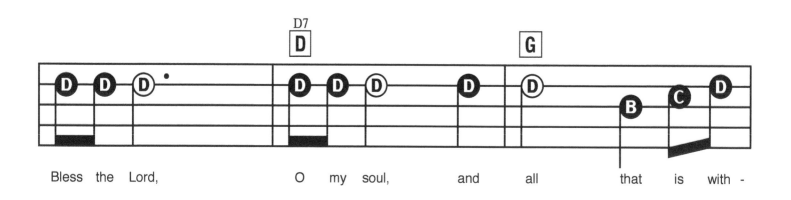

Bless   the   Lord,   O   my   soul,   and   all   that   is   with -

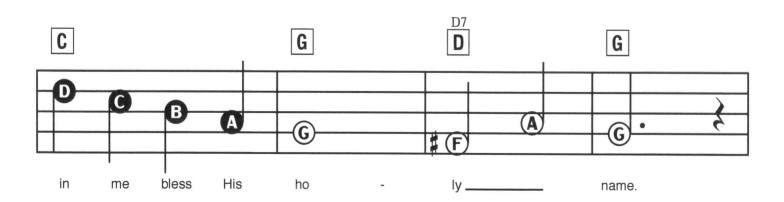

in   me   bless   His   ho   -   ly _____   name.

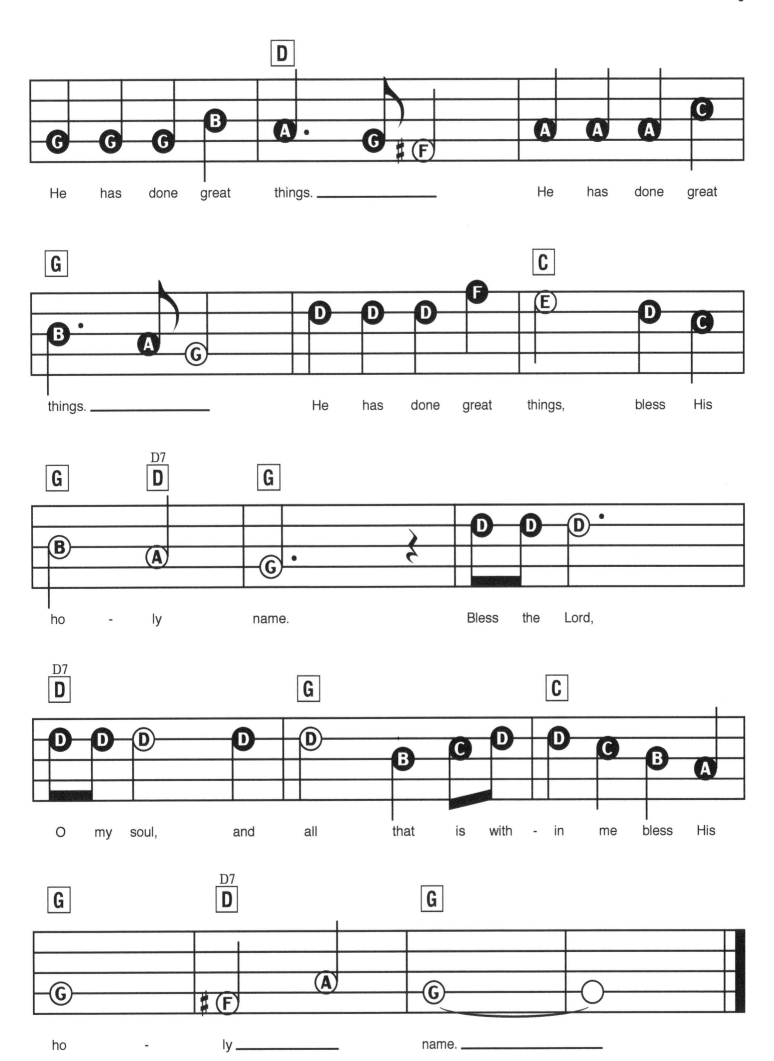

He

Registration 1
Rhythm: Waltz

Words by Richard Mullen
Music by Jack Richards

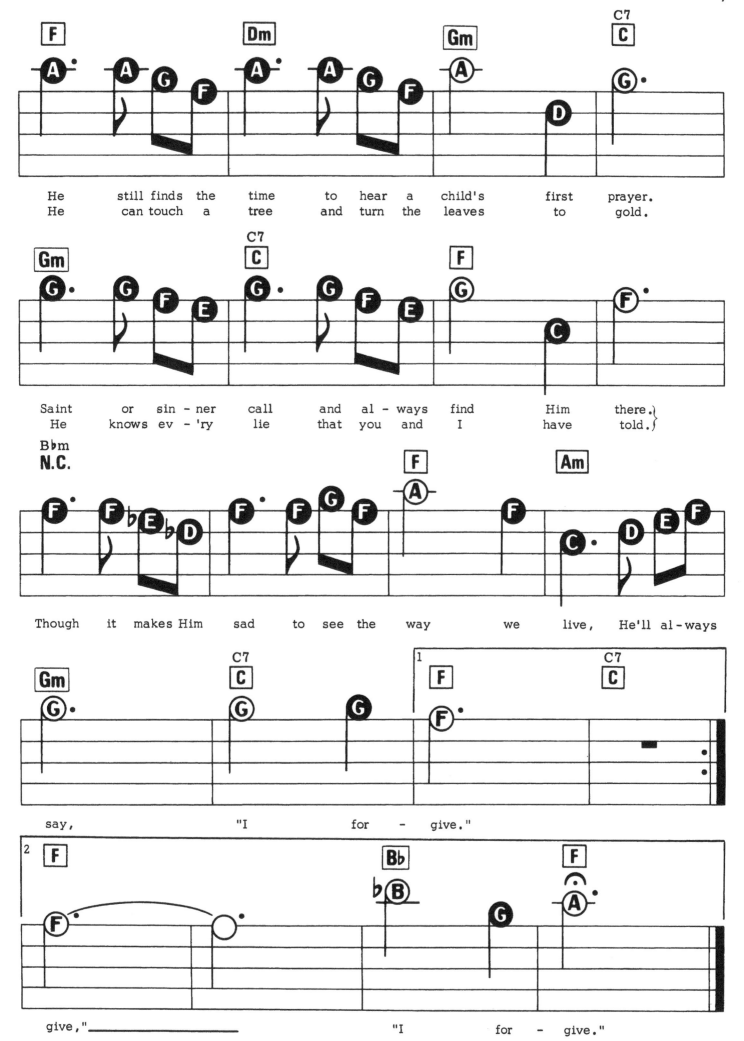

He Lives

Registration 2
Rhythm: 6/8 March

Words and Music by
A.H. Ackley

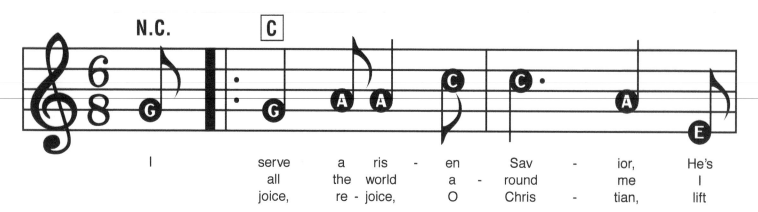

I serve a ris - en Sav - ior, He's
all the world a - round me I
joice, re - joice, O Chris - tian, lift

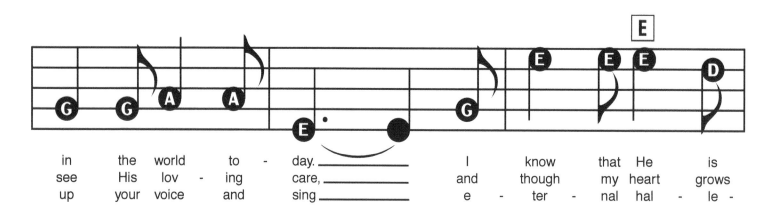

in the world to - day. _____ I know that He is
see His lov - ing care, _____ and know though my heart grows
up your voice and sing _____ e - ter - nal hal - le -

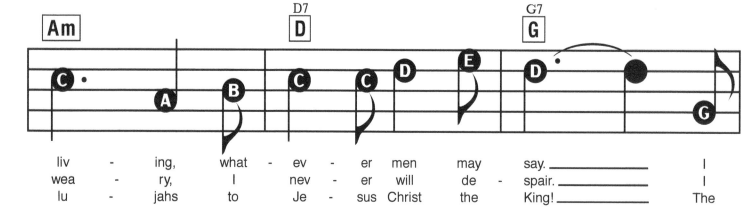

liv - ing, what - ev - er men may say. _____ I
wea - ry, I nev - er will de - spair. _____ I
lu - jahs to Je - sus Christ the King! _____ The

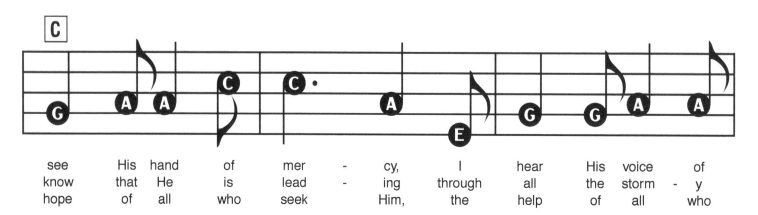

see His hand of mer - cy, I hear His voice of
know that He is lead - ing through all the storm - y
hope of all who seek Him, the help of all who

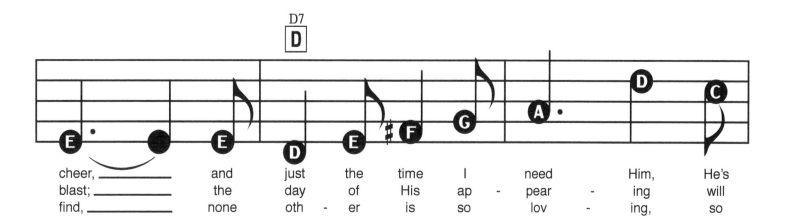

cheer, _____ and just the time I need Him, He's
blast; _____ the day of His ap - pear - ing will
find, _____ none oth - er is so lov - ing, so

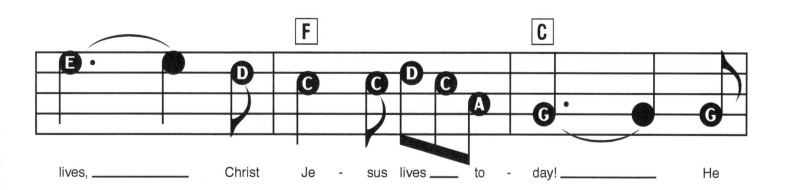

al - ways near. _____ ⎫
come at last. _____ ⎬ He lives, _____ He
good and kind. _____ ⎭

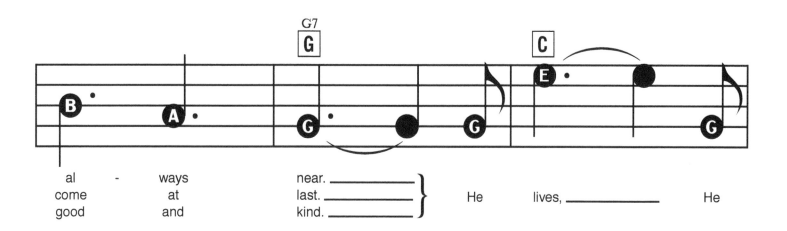

lives, _____ Christ Je - sus lives ___ to - day! _____ He

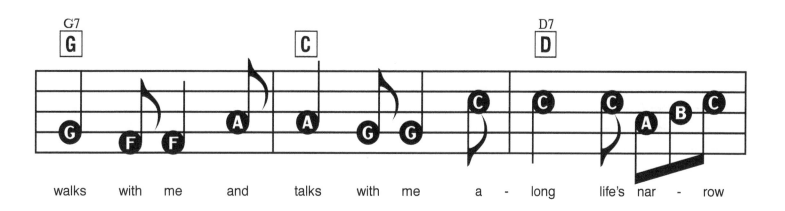

walks with me and talks with me a - long life's nar - row

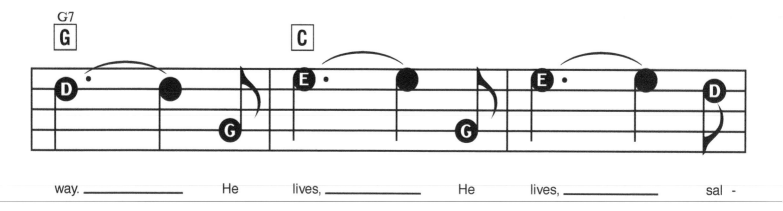

way. _____ He lives, _____ He lives, _____ sal -

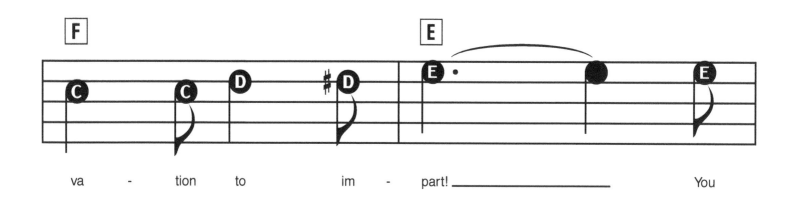

va - tion to im - part! _____ You

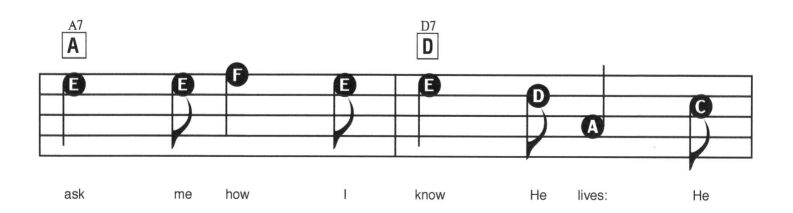

ask me how I know He lives: He

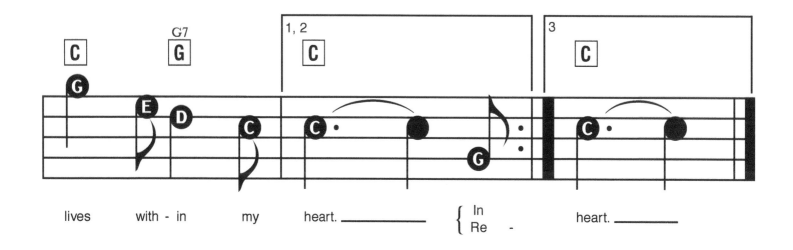

lives with - in my heart. _____ { In / Re - heart. _____

I'll Fly Away

Registration 4
Rhythm: Country or Fox Trot

Words and Music by
Albert E. Brumley

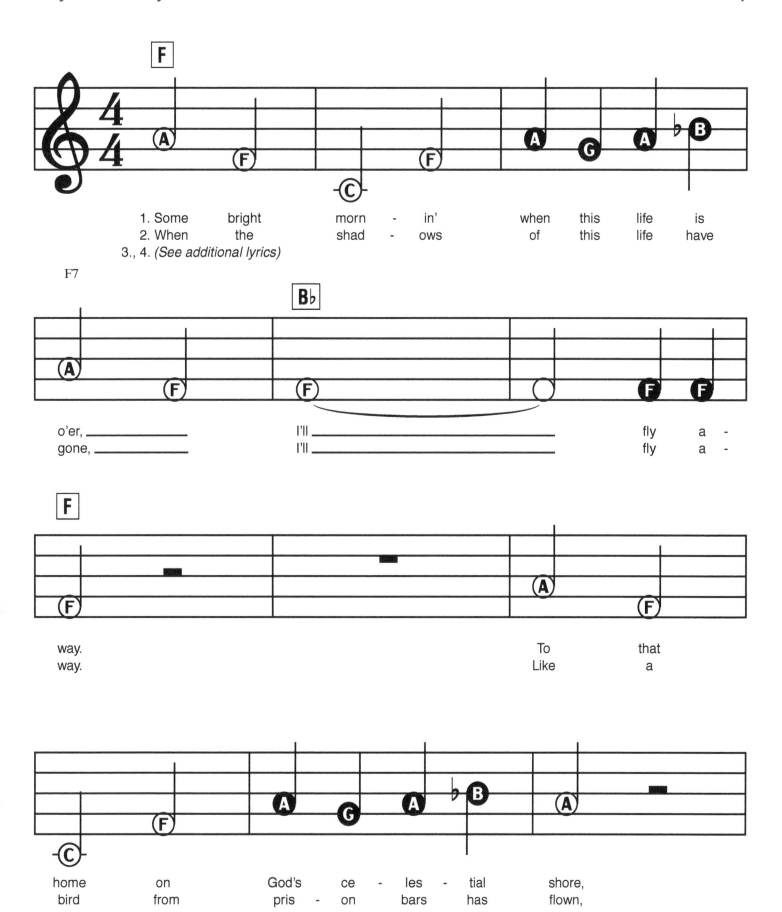

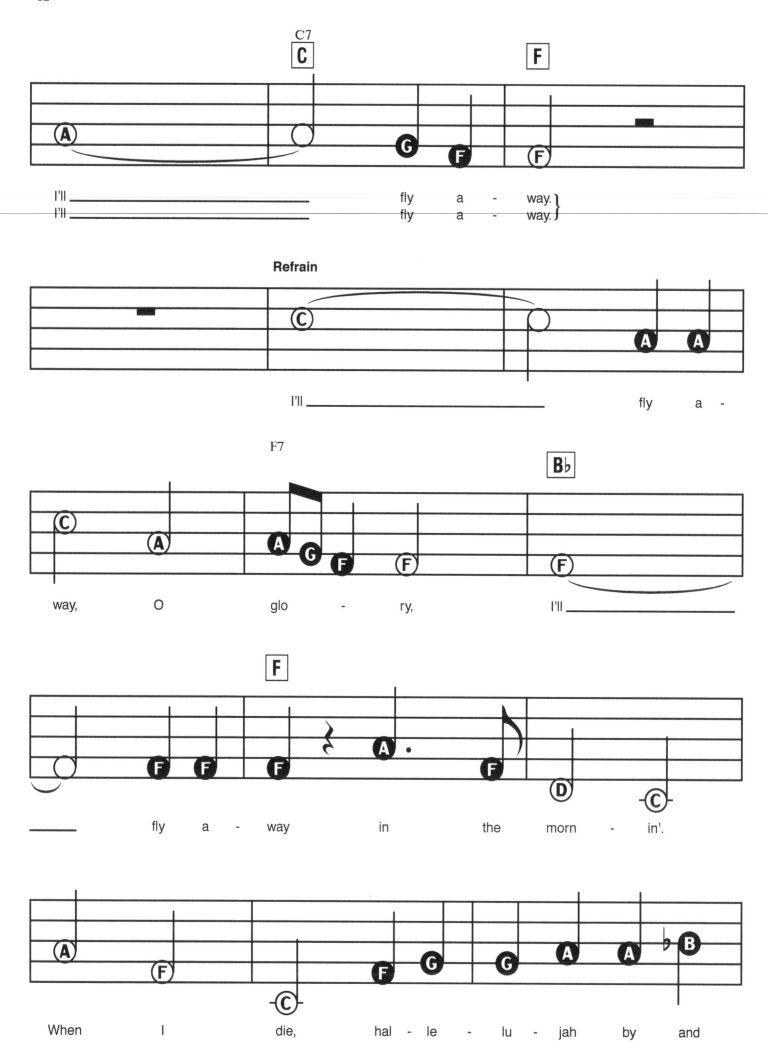

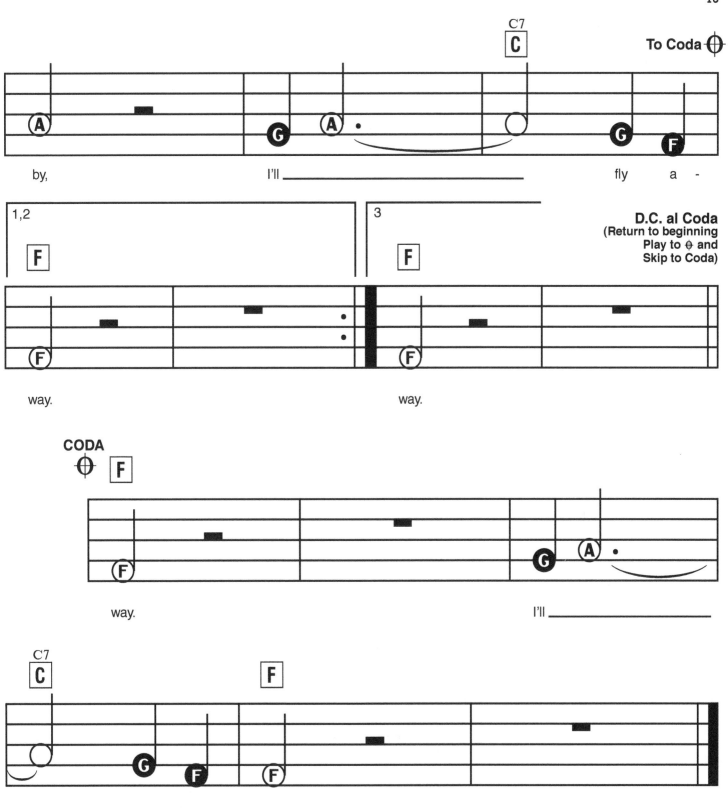

D.C. al Coda
(Return to beginning
Play to ⊕ and
Skip to Coda)

by,   I'll _____   fly a -

way.   way.

way.   I'll _____

____   fly a - way.

Additional Lyrics

3. Oh, how glad and happy when we meet,
   I'll fly away.
   No more cold iron shackles on my feet,
   I'll fly away.
   Refrain

4. Just a few more weary days and then
   I'll fly away
   To a land where joys will never end,
   I'll fly away.
   Refrain

He Touched Me

Registration 2
Rhythm: Waltz

Words and Music by
William J. Gaither

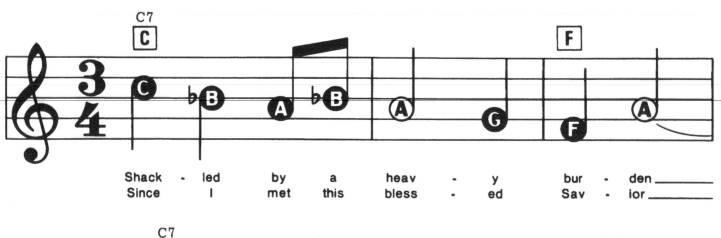

Shack - led by a heav - y bur - den _____
Since I met this bless - ed Sav - ior _____

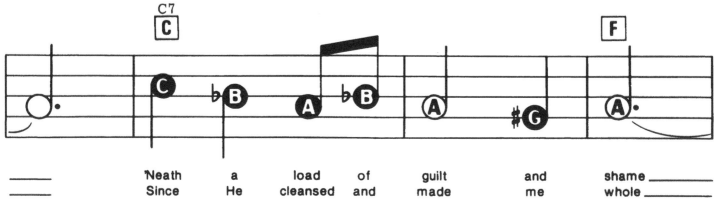

_____ 'Neath a load of guilt and shame _____
Since He cleansed and made me whole _____

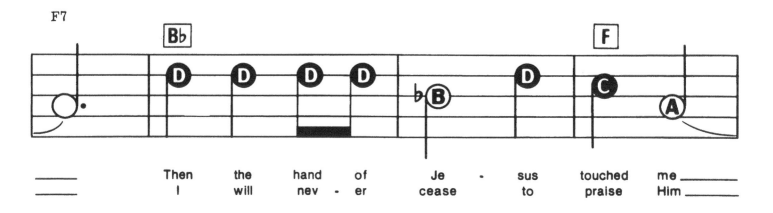

_____ Then the hand of Je - sus touched me _____
_____ I will nev - er cease to praise Him _____

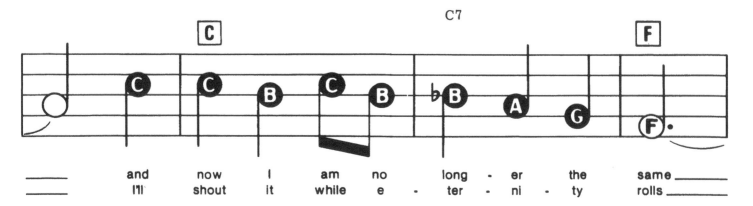

_____ and now I am no long - er the same _____
I'll shout it while e - ter - ni - ty rolls _____

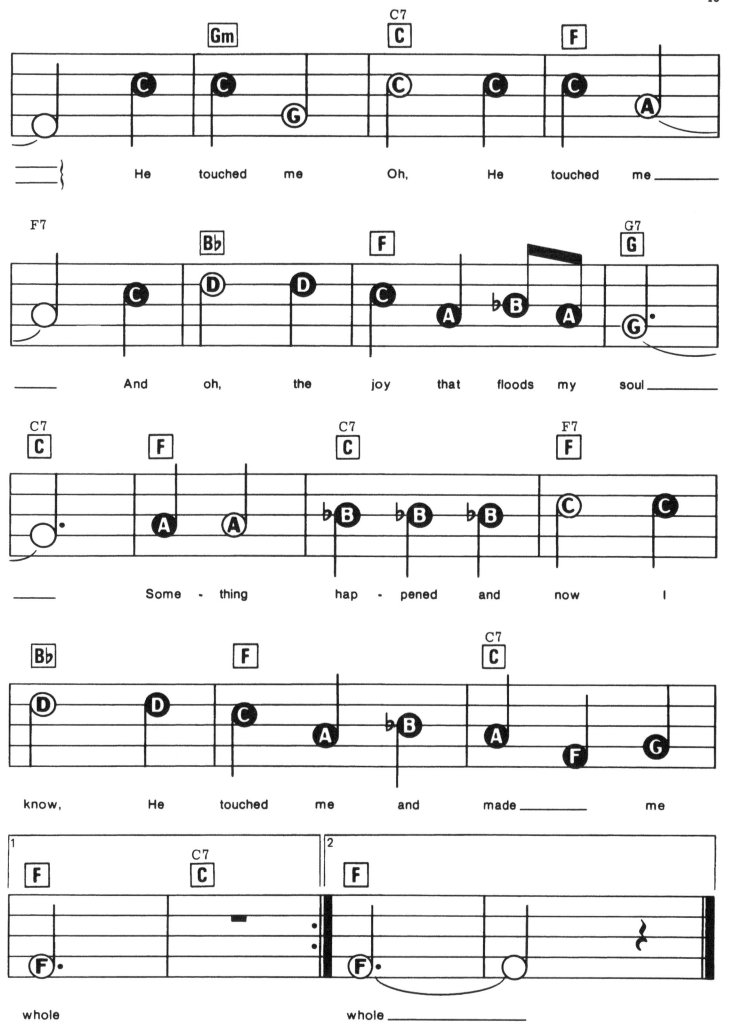

His Eye Is on the Sparrow

Registration 3
Rhythm: Waltz

Words by Civilla D. Martin
Music by Charles H. Gabriel

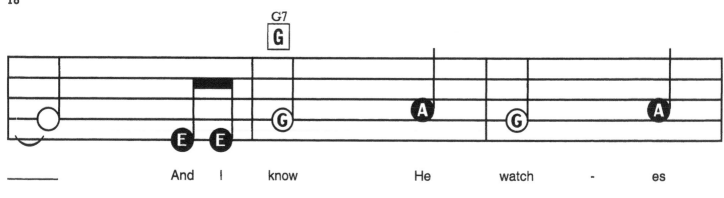

And I know He watch - es

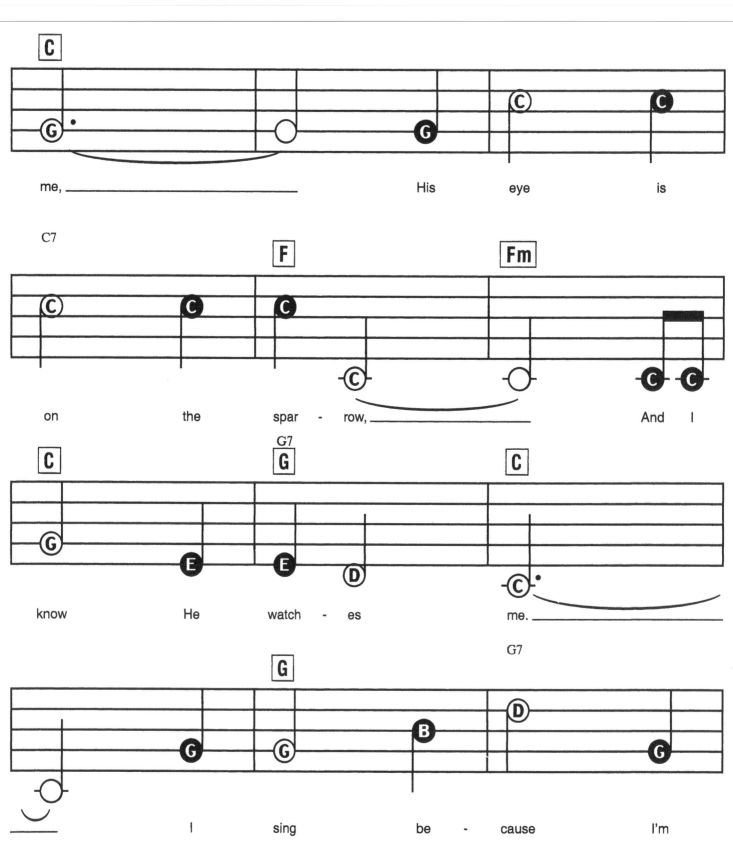

me, _____ His eye is

on the spar - row, _____ And I

know He watch - es me. _____

I sing be - cause I'm

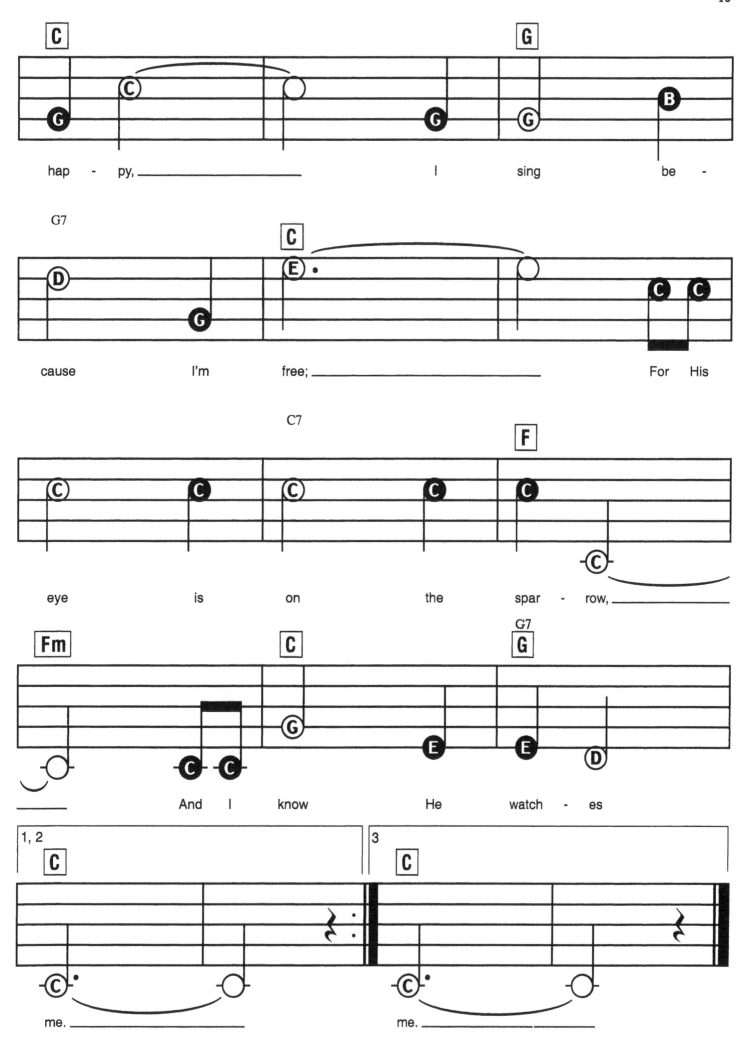

How Great Thou Art

Registration 6
Rhythm: Ballad

Words and Music by
Stuart K. Hine

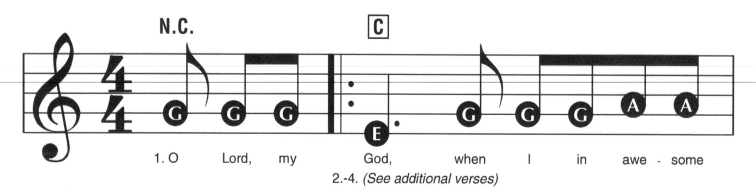

1. O Lord, my God, when I in awe - some

2.-4. *(See additional verses)*

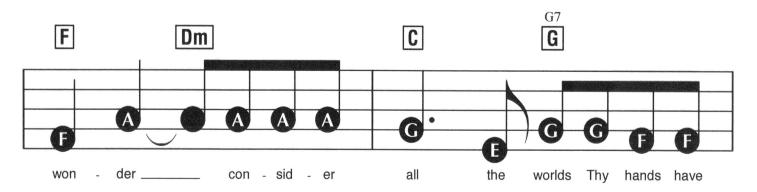

won - der _____ con - sid - er all the worlds Thy hands have

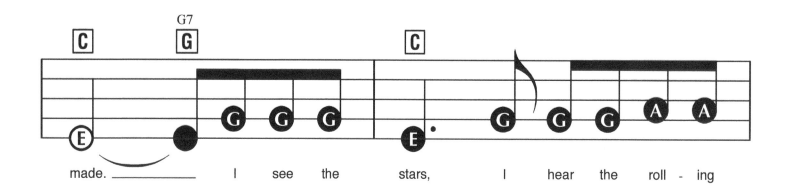

made. _____ I see the stars, I hear the roll - ing

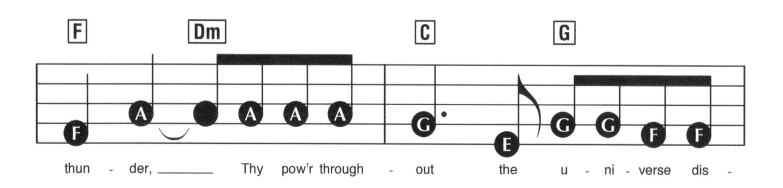

thun - der, _____ Thy pow'r through - out the u - ni - verse dis -

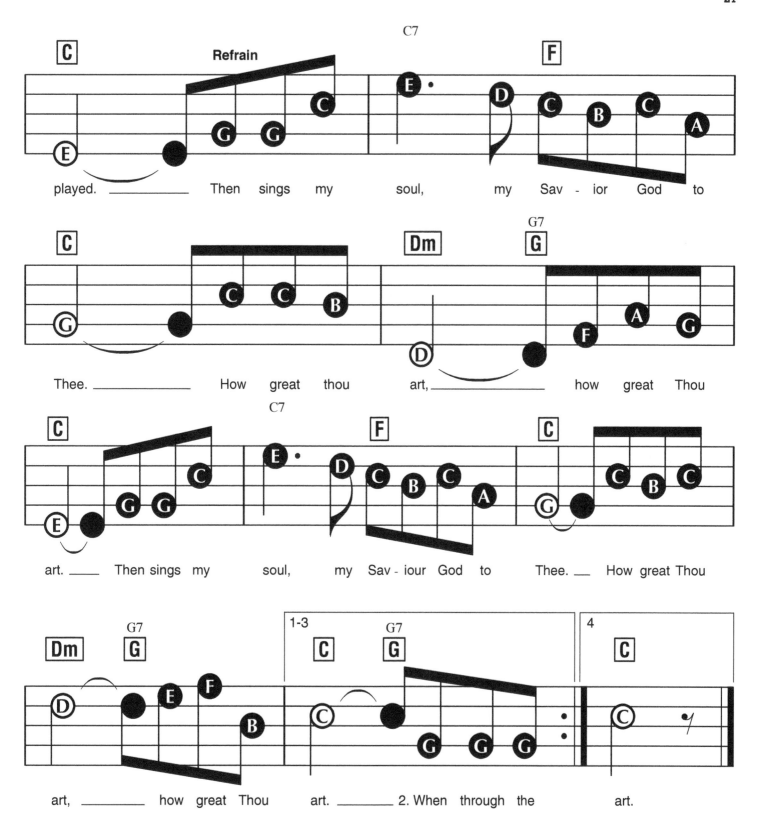

Additional Verses

2. When through the woods and forest glades I wander,
   And hear the birds sing sweetly in the trees.
   When I look down from lofty mountain grandeur,
   And hear the brook and feel the gentle breeze.
   Refrain

3. And when I think that God His Son not sparing,
   Sent Him to die, I scarce can take it in.
   That on the cross, my burden gladly bearing,
   He bled and died to take away my sin.
   Refrain

4. When Christ shall come with shout of acclamation
   And take me home, what joy shall fill my heart!
   Then I shall bow in humble adoration
   And there proclaim my God how great Thou art.
   Refrain

I Saw the Light

Registration 4
Rhythm: Fox Trot or Country

Words and Music by
Hank Williams

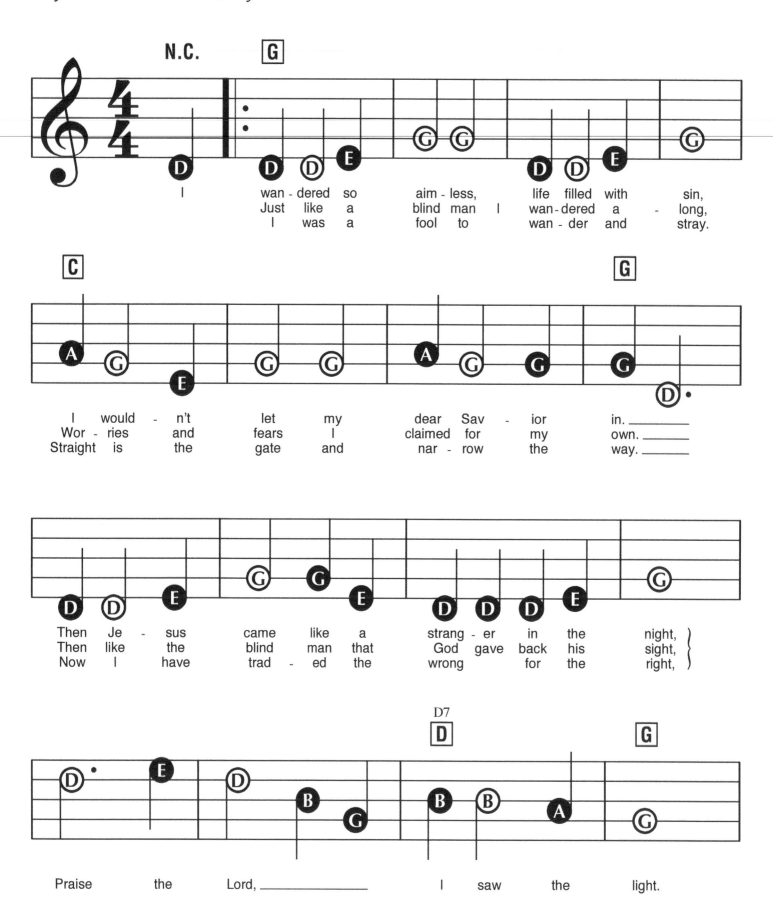

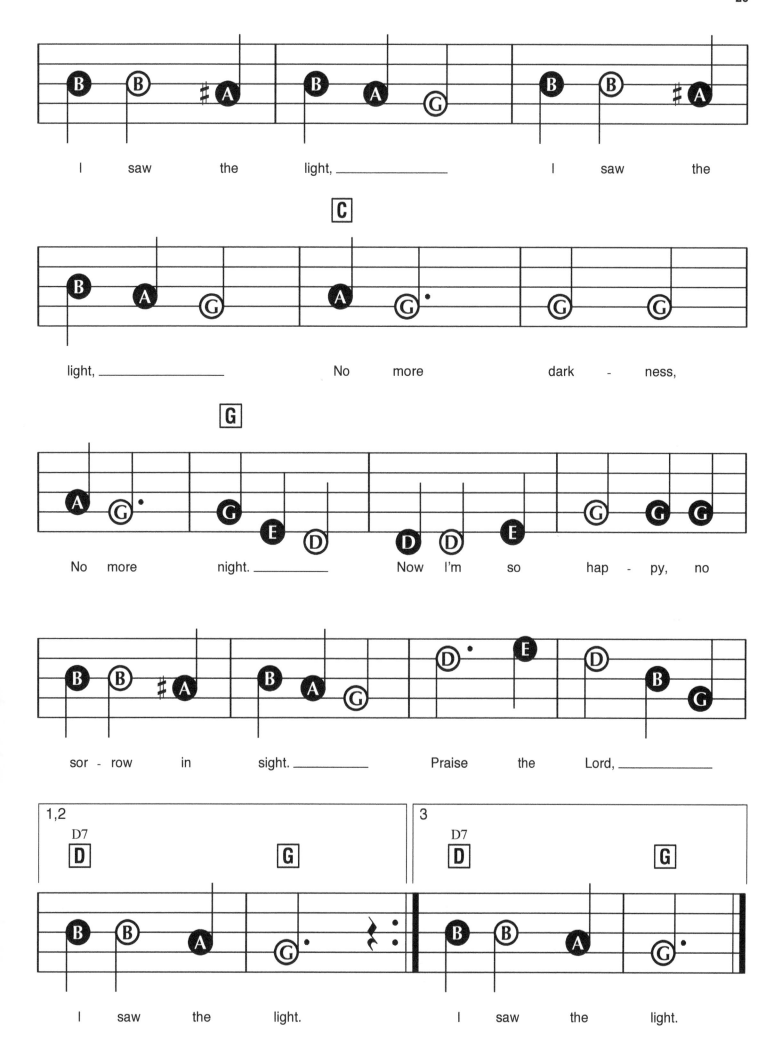

In the Garden

Registration 1
Rhythm: Waltz

Words and Music by
C. Austin Miles

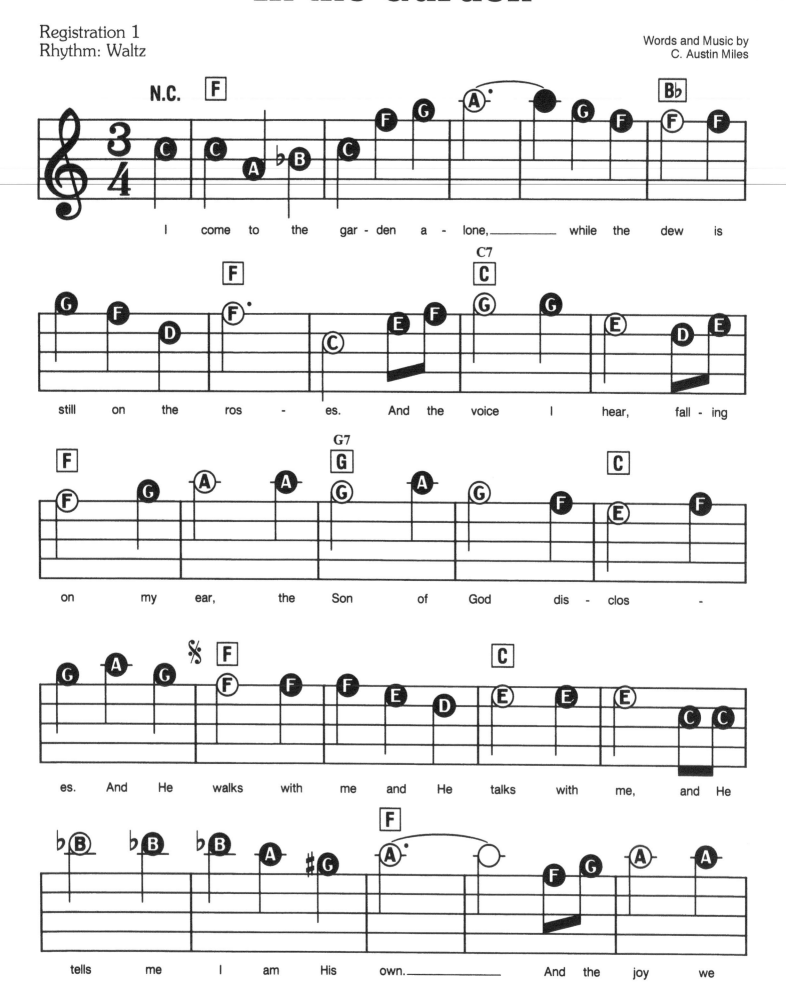

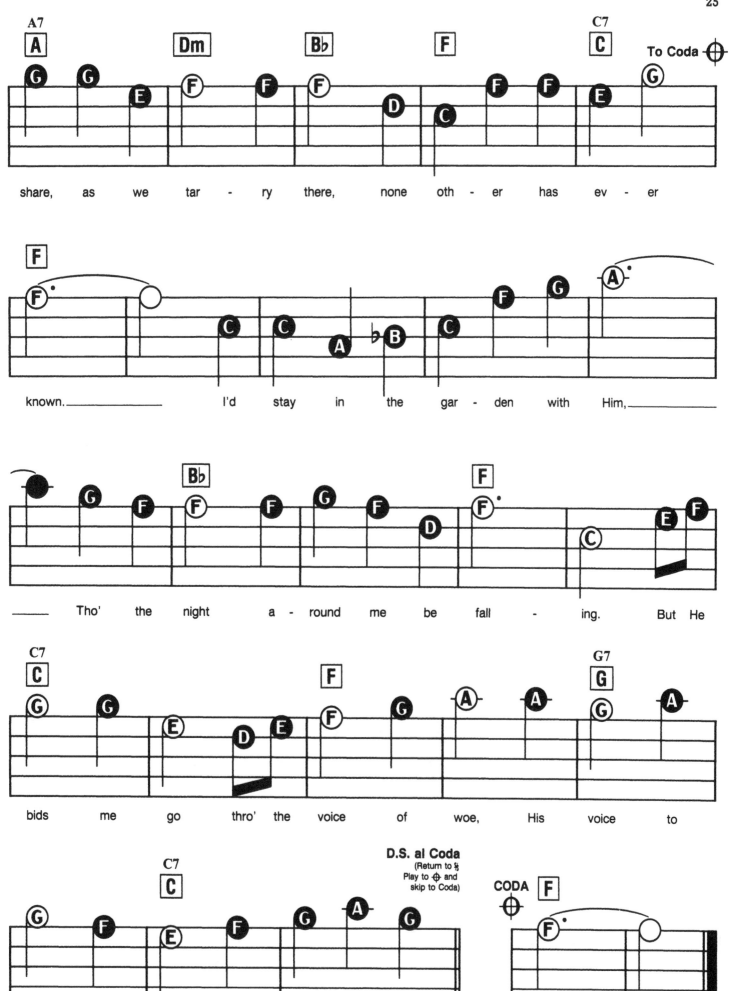

It Is No Secret
(What God Can Do)

Registration 4
Rhythm: Country

Words and Music by
Stuart Hamblen

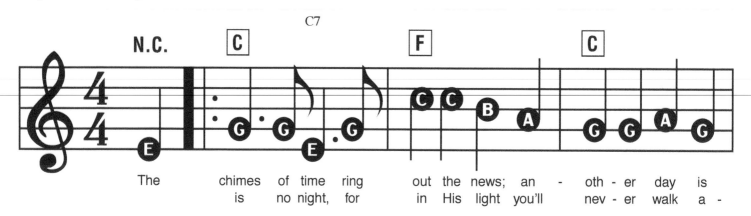

The chimes of time ring out the news; an - oth - er day is
is no night, for in His light you'll nev - er walk a -

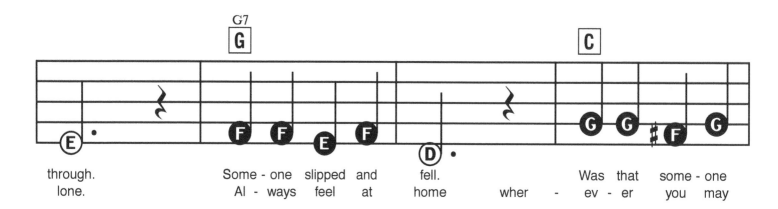

through. Some - one slipped and fell. Was that some - one
lone. Al - ways feel at home wher - ev - er you may

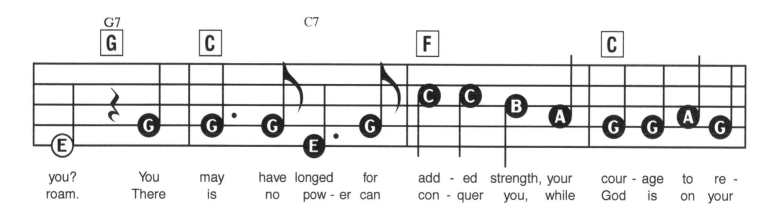

you? You may have longed for add - ed strength, your cour - age to re -
roam. There is no pow - er can con - quer you, while God is on your

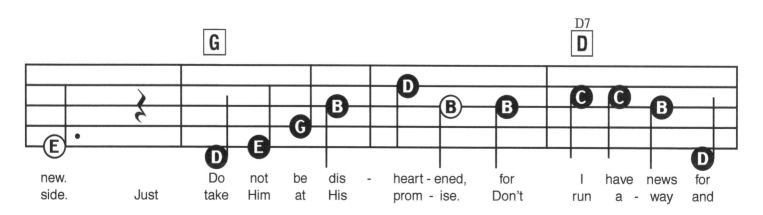

new. Do not be dis - heart - ened, for I have news for
side. Just take Him at His prom - ise. Don't run a - way and

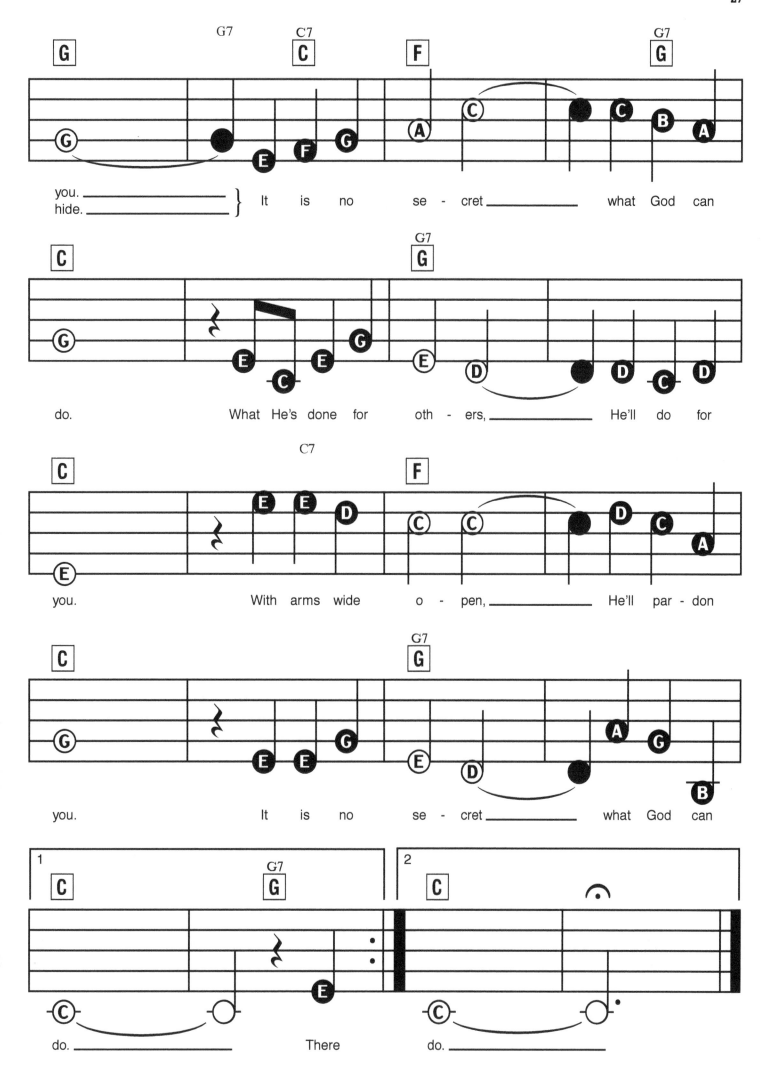

Just a Closer Walk with Thee

Registration 2
Rhythm: Country Swing

Traditional

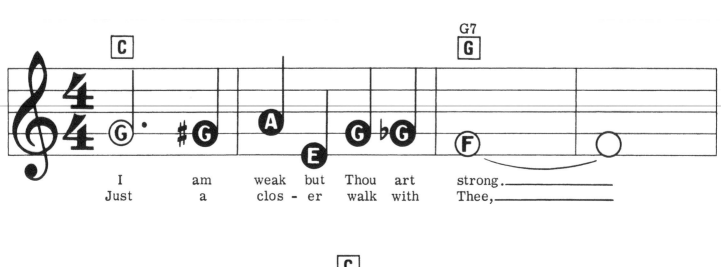

I am weak but Thou art strong._____
Just a clos - er walk with Thee,_____

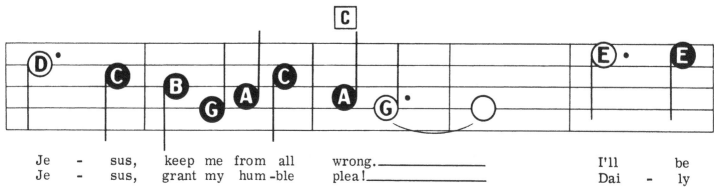

Je - sus, keep me from all wrong._____ I'll be
Je - sus, grant my hum -ble plea!_____ Dai - ly

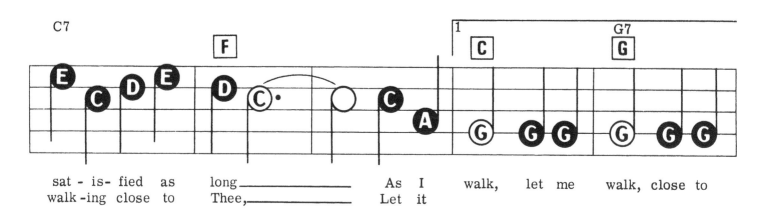

sat - is- fied as long_____ As I walk, let me walk, close to
walk -ing close to Thee,_____ Let it

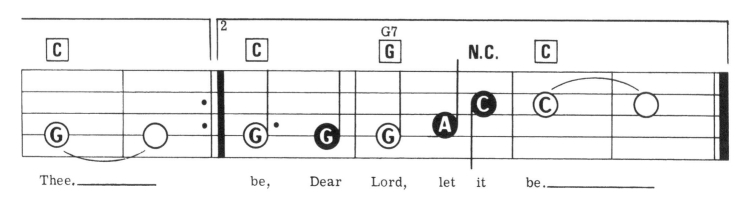

Thee._____ be, Dear Lord, let it be._____

Turn Your Radio On

Registration 4
Rhythm: Fox Trot or Country

Words and Music by
Albert E. Brumley

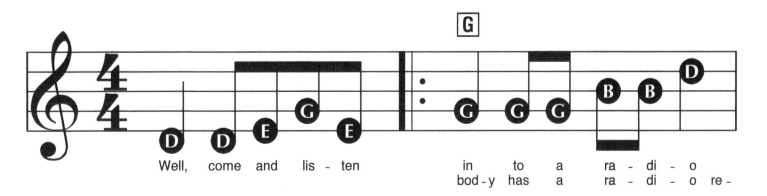

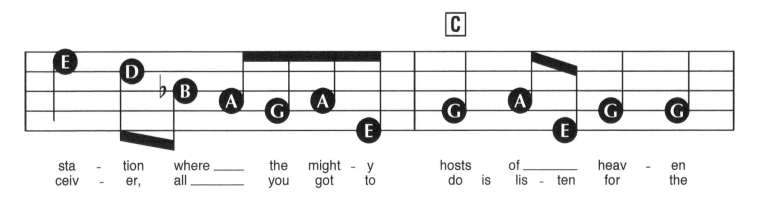

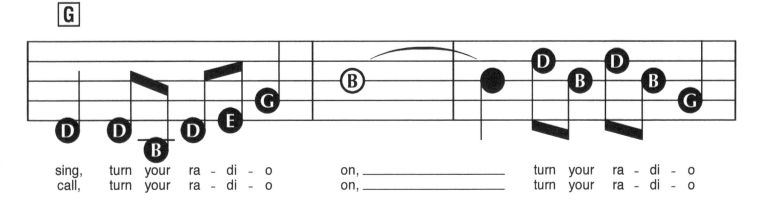

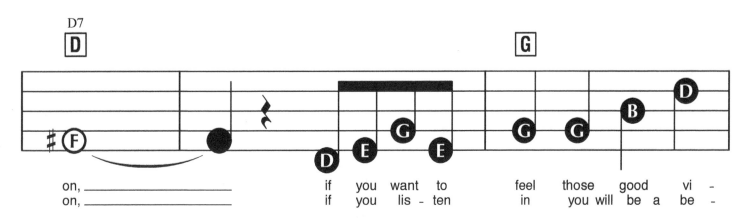

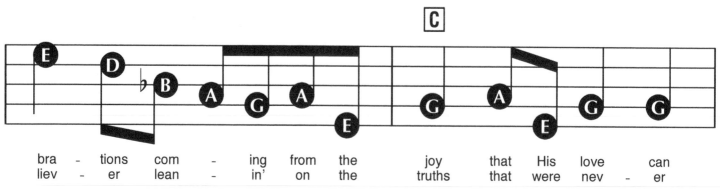

bra - tions com - ing from the   joy   that His love can
liev - er lean - in' on the   truths that His were nev - er

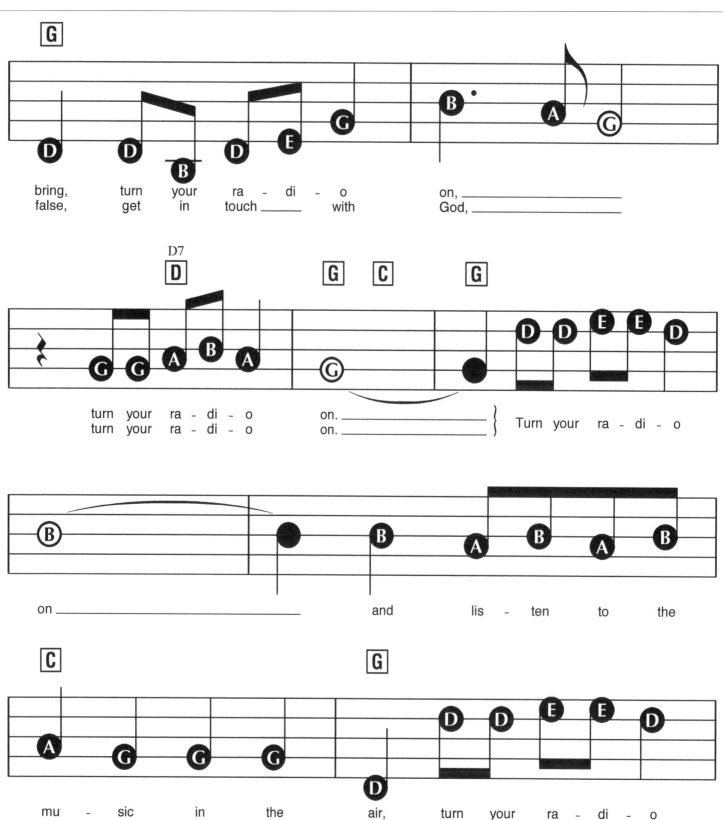

bring, turn your ra - di - o   on, _____
false, get in touch ____ with   God, _____

turn your ra - di - o   on. _____   Turn your ra - di - o
turn your ra - di - o   on. _____

on _____ and lis - ten to the

mu - sic in the air, turn your ra - di - o

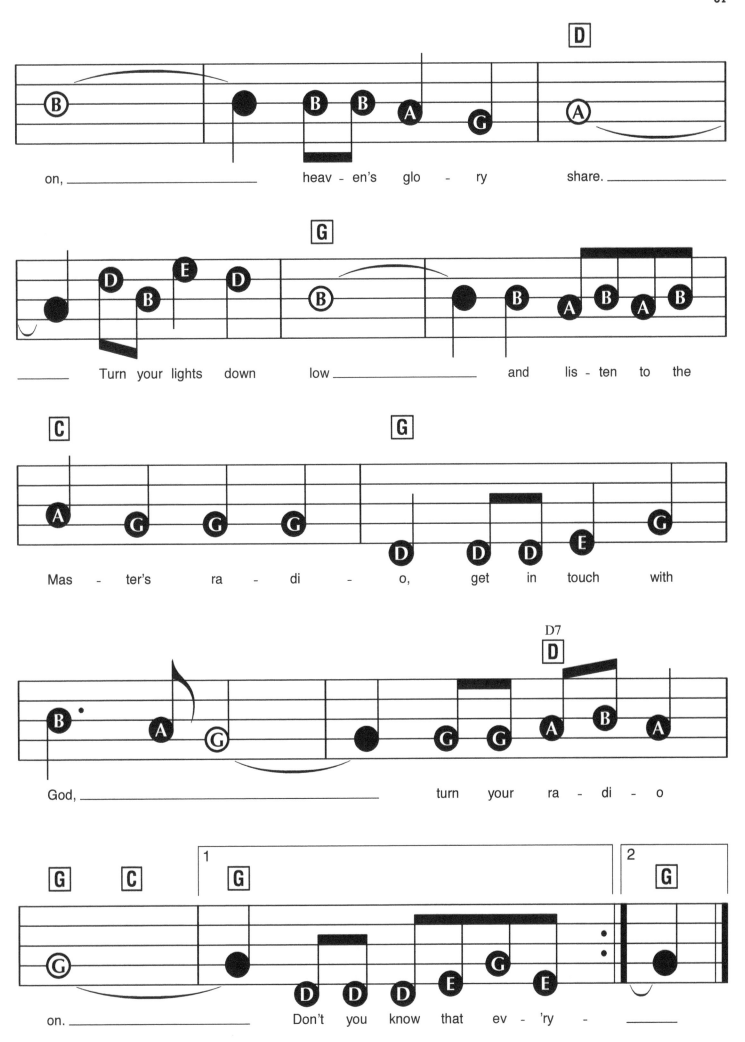

The King Is Coming

Registration 6
Rhythm: Waltz

Words by William J. and Gloria Gaither and Charles Millhuff
Music by William J. Gaither

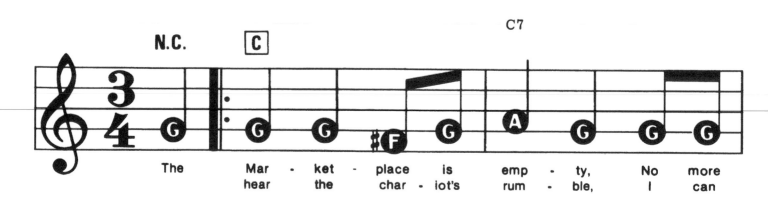

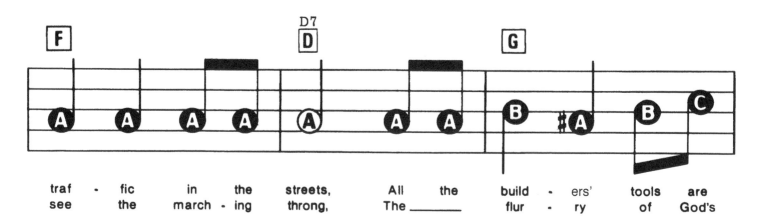

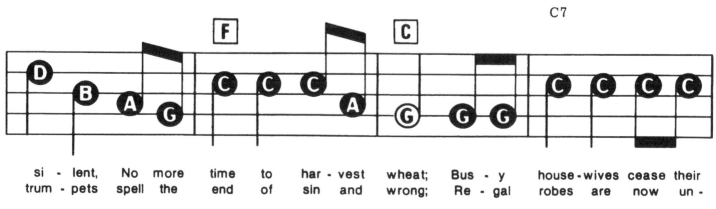

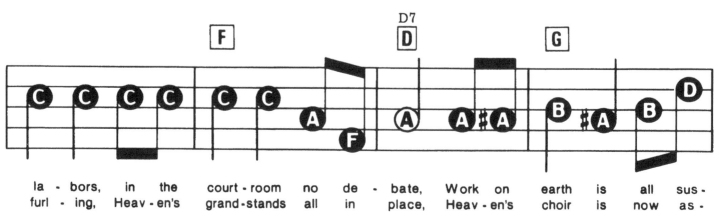

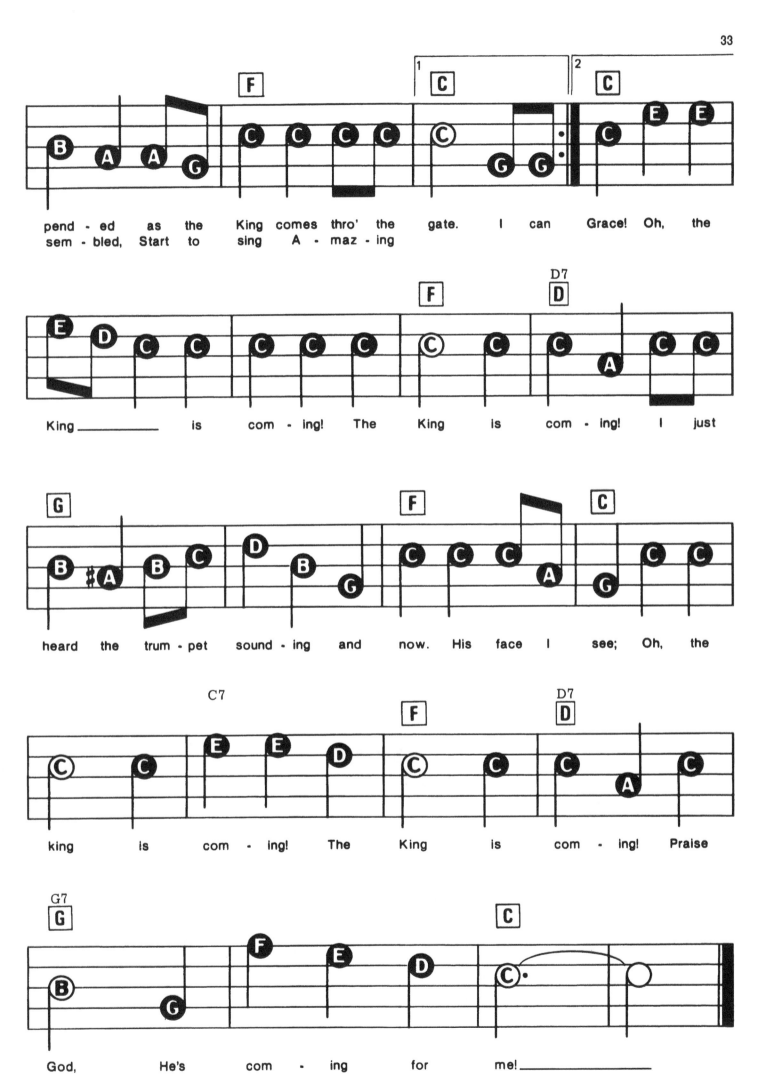

Mansion Over the Hilltop

Registration 4
Rhythm: Country Swing

Words and Music by
Ira F. Stanphill

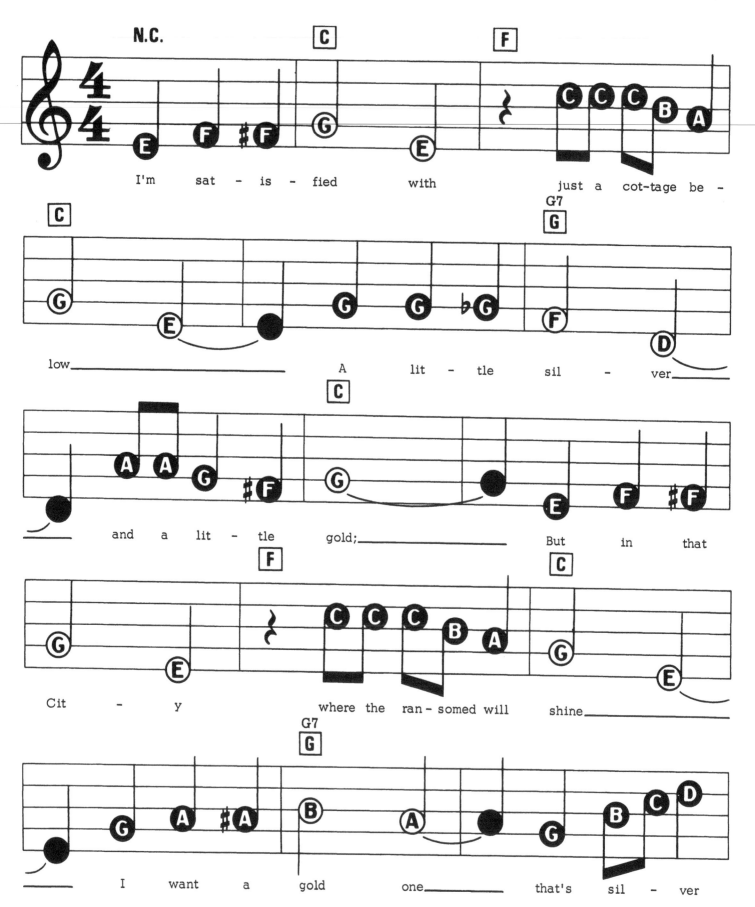

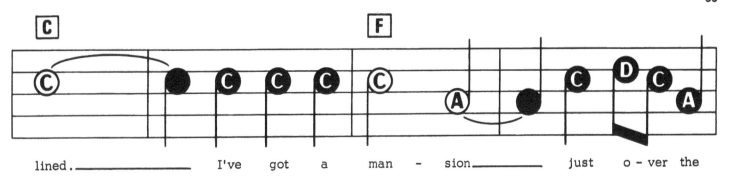

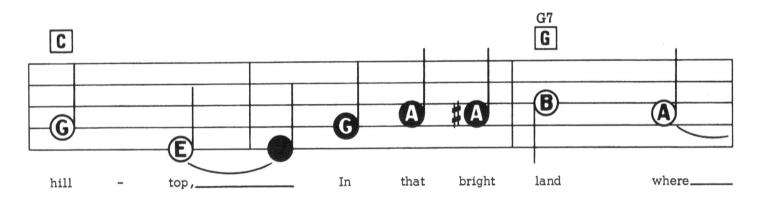

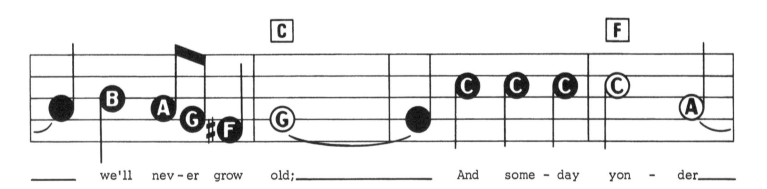

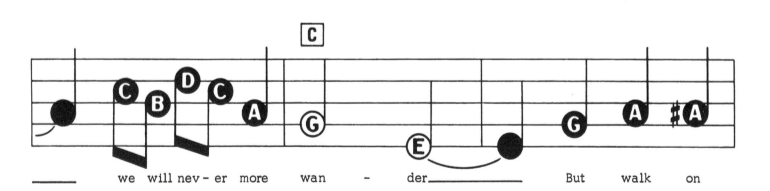

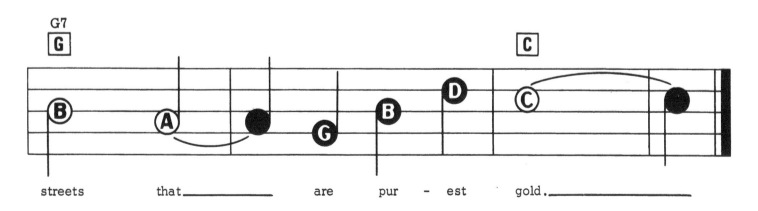

My Tribute

Registration 1
Rhythm: Ballad or 8-Beat

Words and Music by
Andraé Crouch

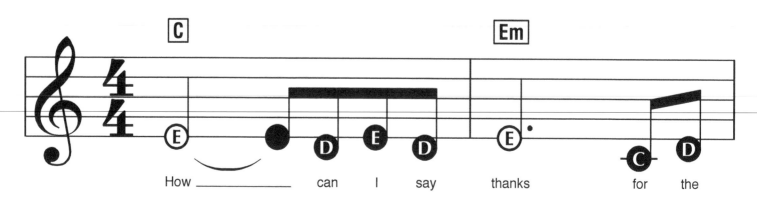

How _____ can I say thanks for the

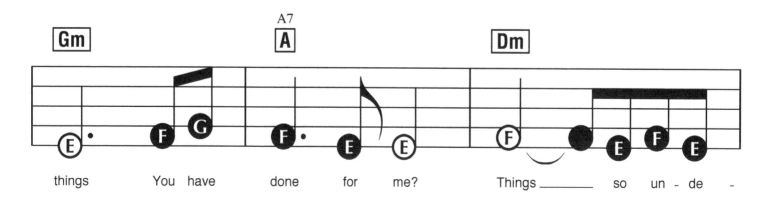

things You have done for me? Things _____ so un - de -

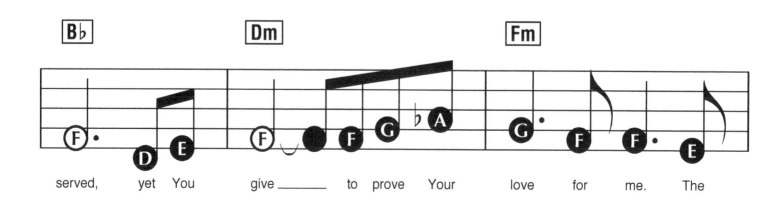

served, yet You give _____ to prove Your love for me. The

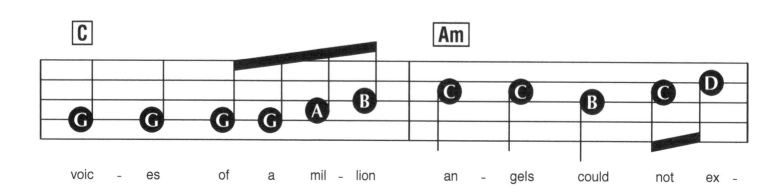

voic - es of a mil - lion an - gels could not ex -

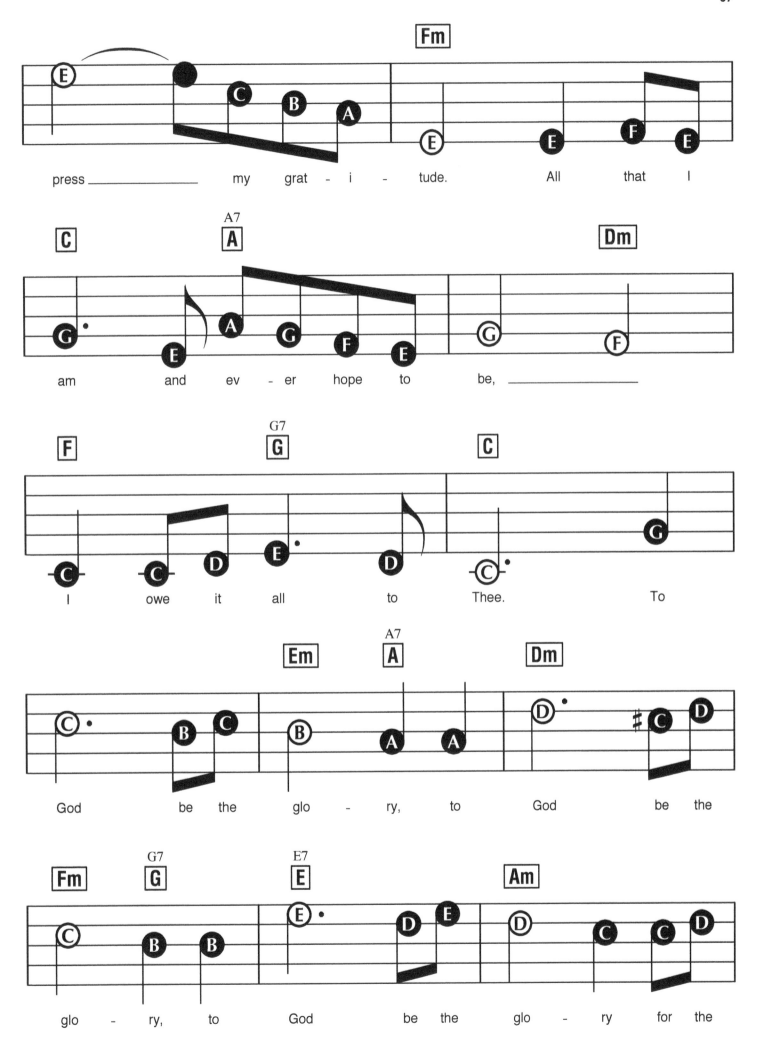

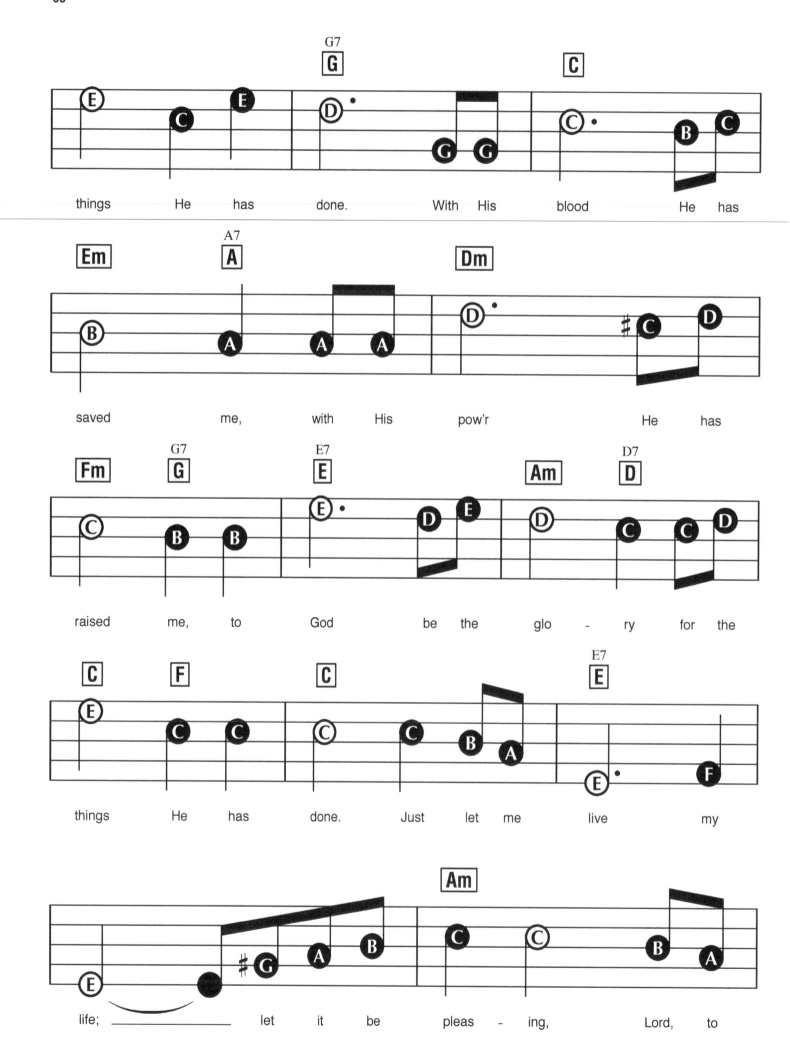

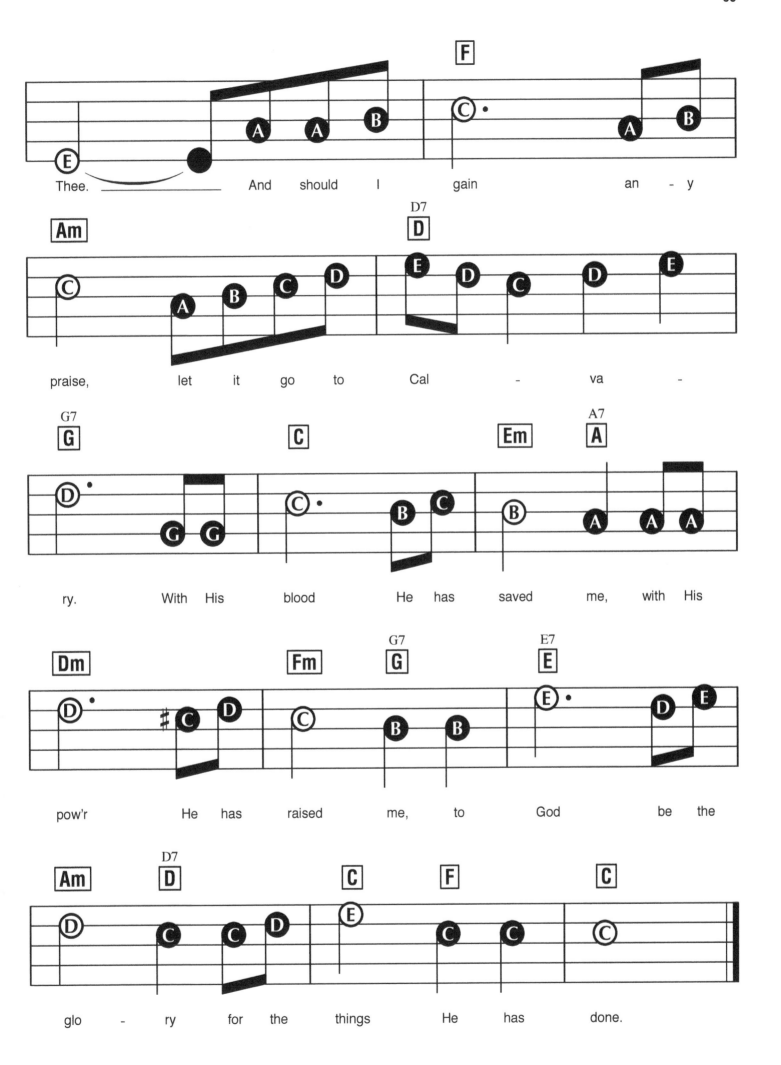

The Old Rugged Cross

Registration 2
Rhythm: Waltz

Words and Music by
Rev. George Bennard

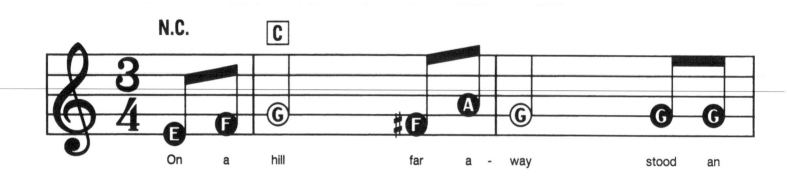

On a hill far a - way stood an

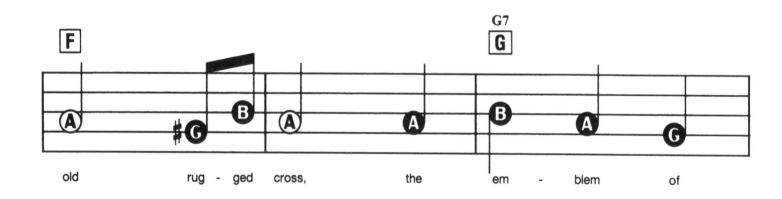

old rug - ged cross, the em - blem of

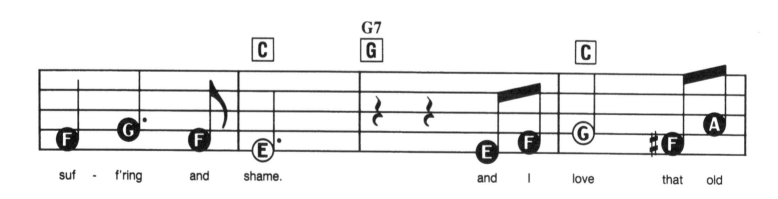

suf - f'ring and shame. and I love that old

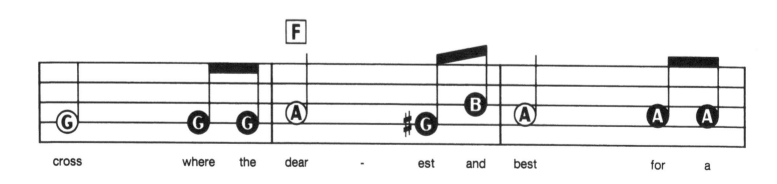

cross where the dear - est and best for a

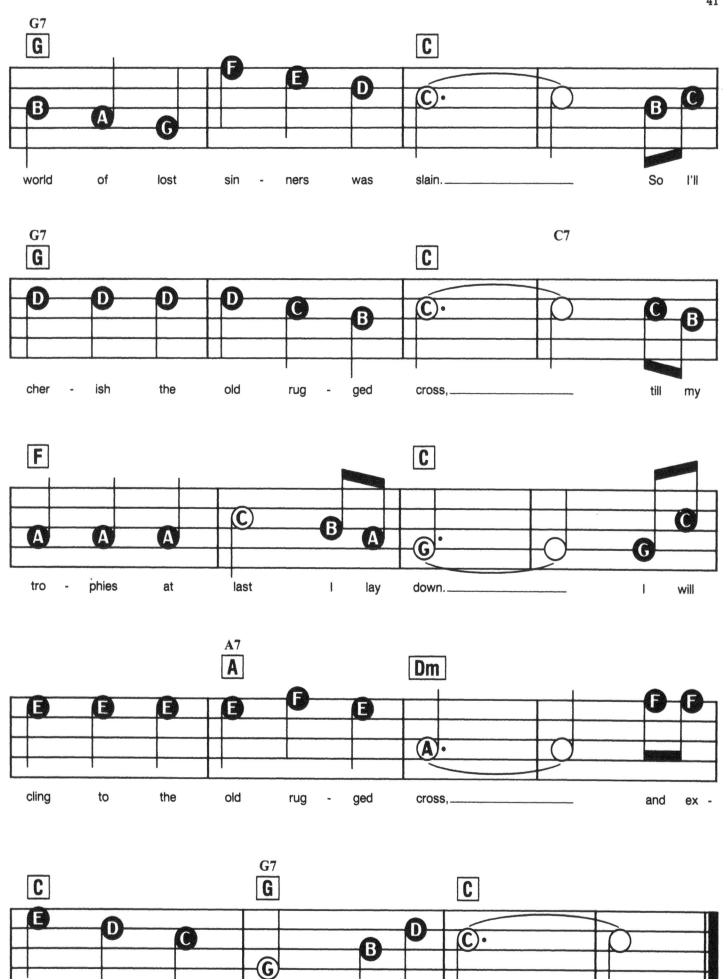

Precious Lord, Take My Hand
(Take My Hand, Precious Lord)

Registration 1
Rhythm: Waltz

Words and Music by
Thomas A. Dorsey

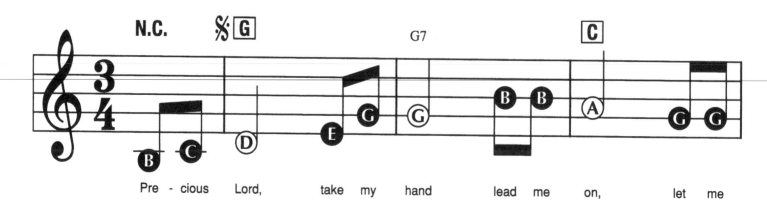

Pre - cious Lord, take my hand lead me on, let me

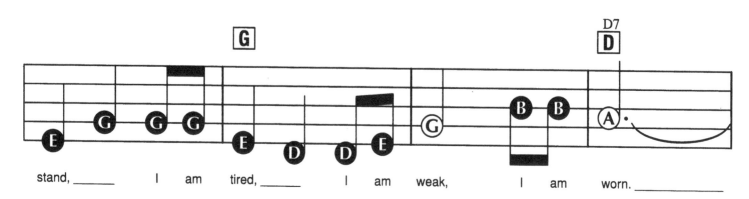

stand, _____ I am tired, _____ I am weak, I am worn. _____

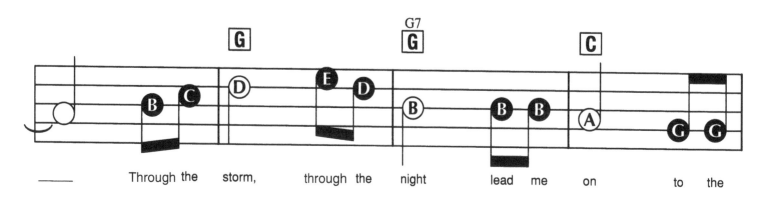

_____ Through the storm, through the night lead me on to the

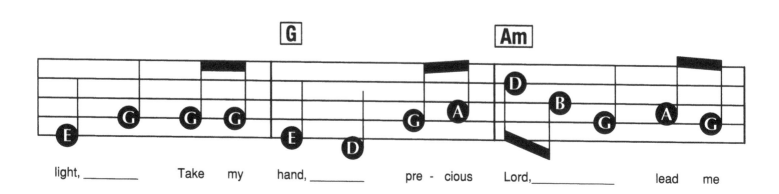

light, _____ Take my hand, _____ pre - cious Lord, _____ lead me

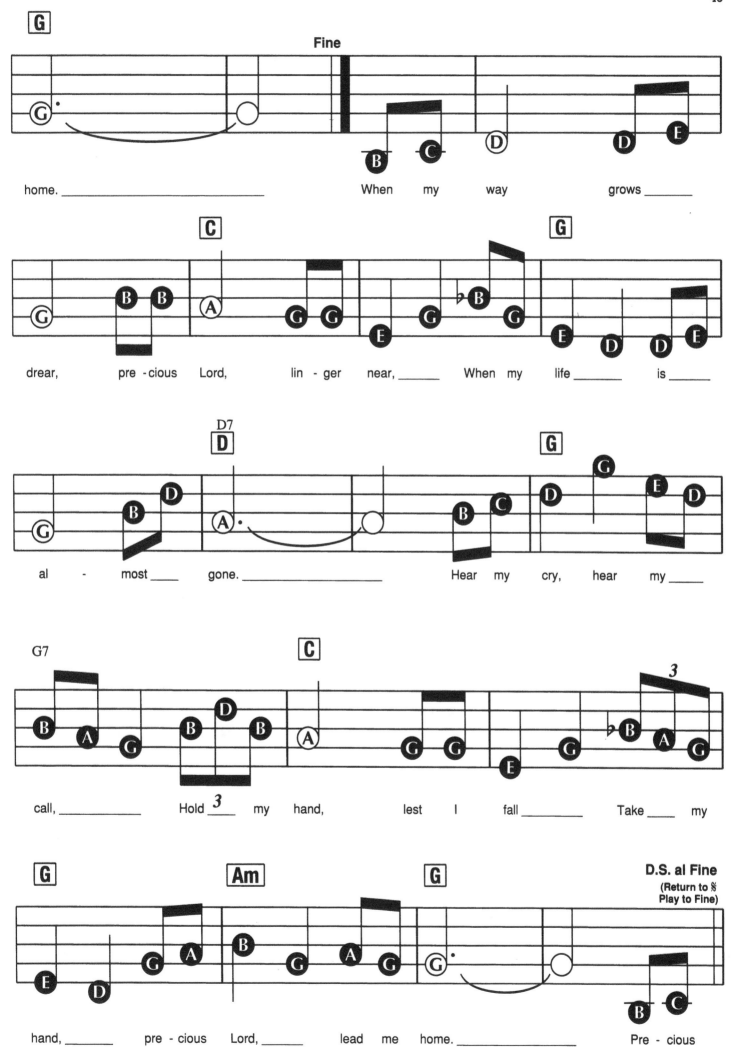

Precious Memories

Registration 2
Rhythm: Swing or Ballad

Words and Music by
J.B.F. Wright

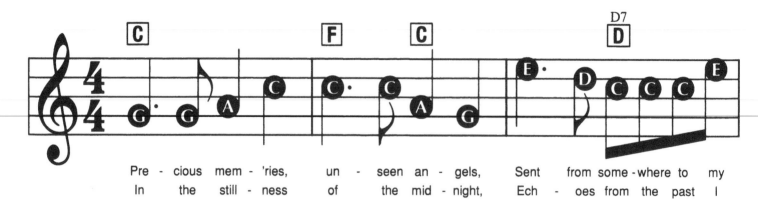

Pre - cious mem - 'ries, un - seen an - gels, Sent from some - where to my
In the still - ness of the mid - night, Ech - oes from the past I

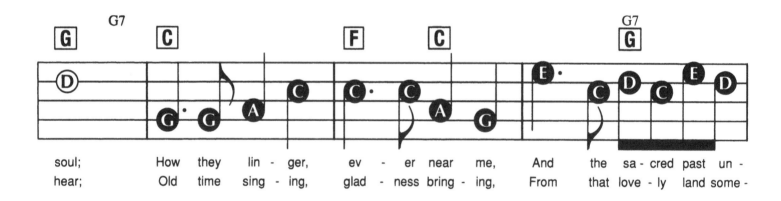

soul; How they lin - ger, ev - er near me, And the sa - cred past un -
hear; Old time sing - ing, glad - ness bring - ing, From that love - ly land some -

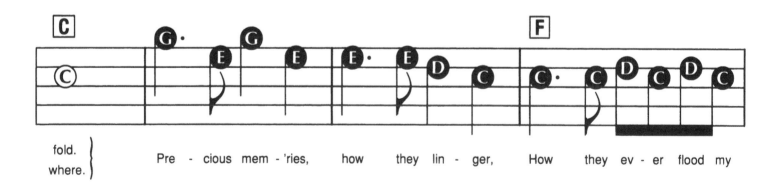

fold. }
where. }
Pre - cious mem - 'ries, how they lin - ger, How they ev - er flood my

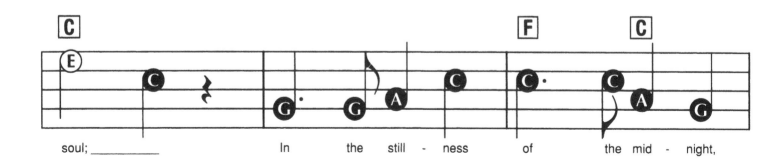

soul; _____ In the still - ness of the mid - night,

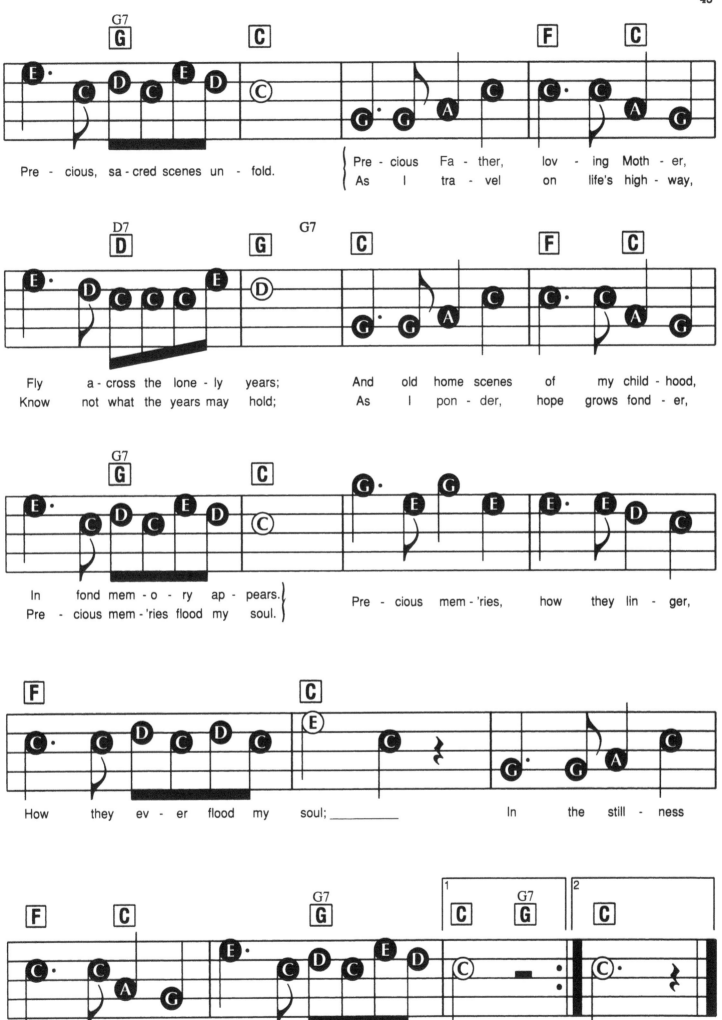

Victory in Jesus

Registration 4
Rhythm: Gospel or Country

Words and Music by
E.M. Bartlett

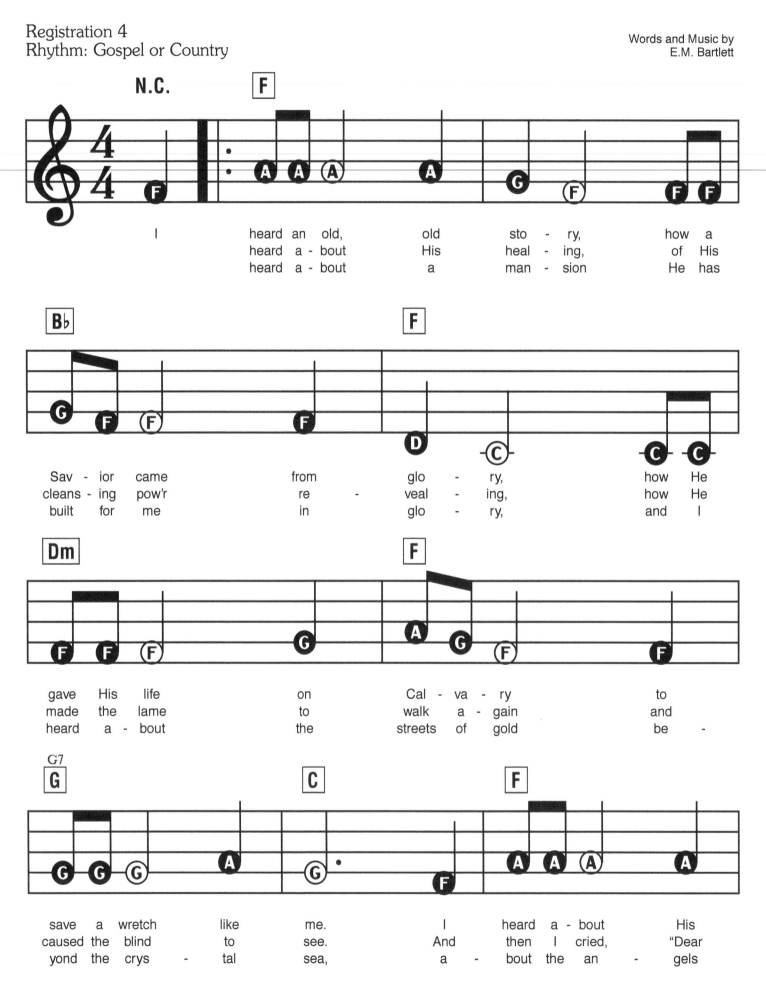

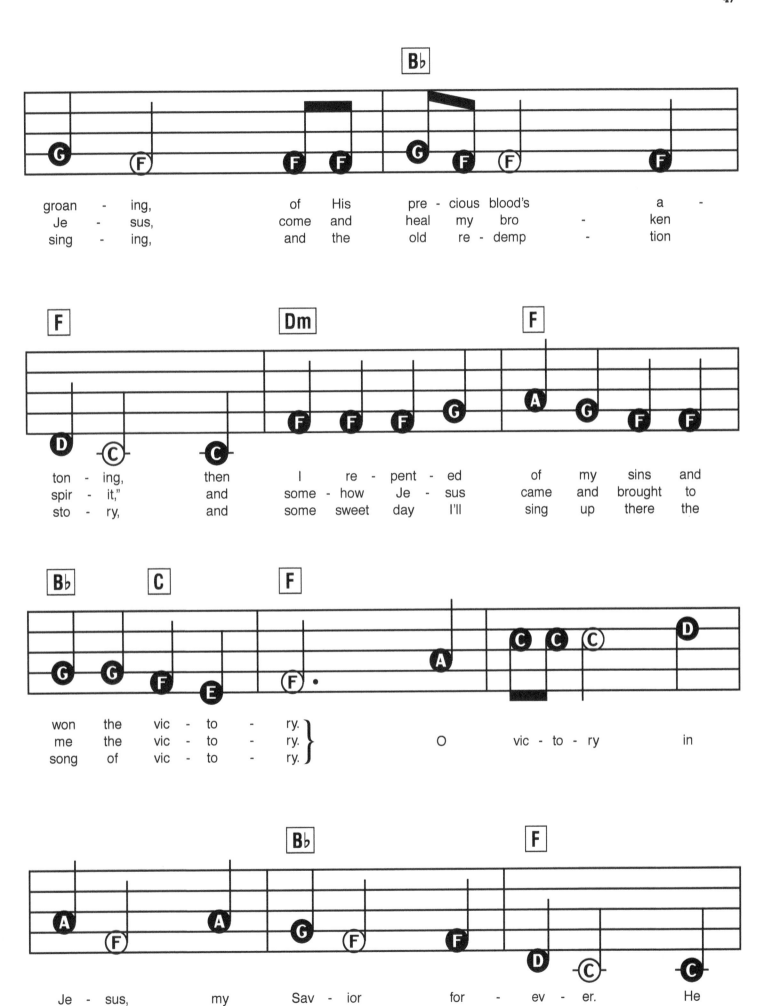

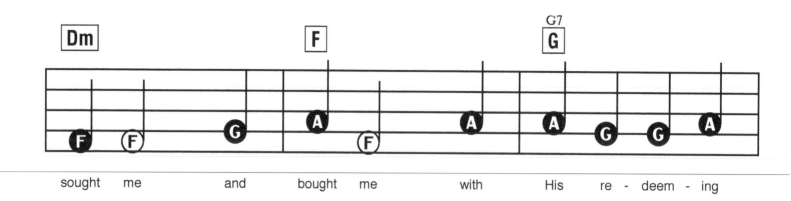

sought me and bought me with His re - deem - ing

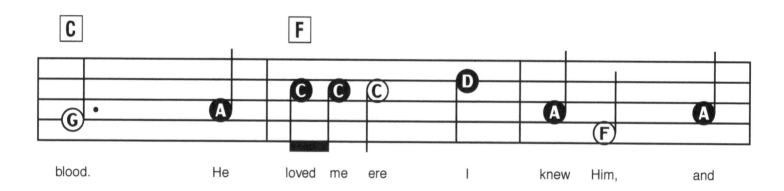

blood. He loved me ere I knew Him, and

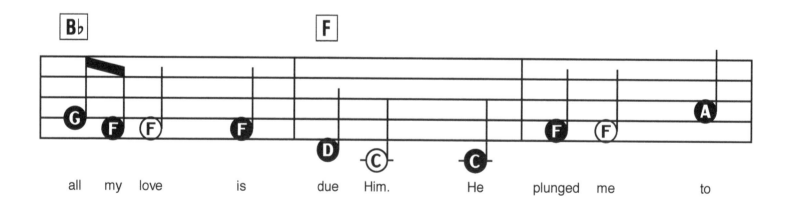

all my love is due Him. He plunged me to

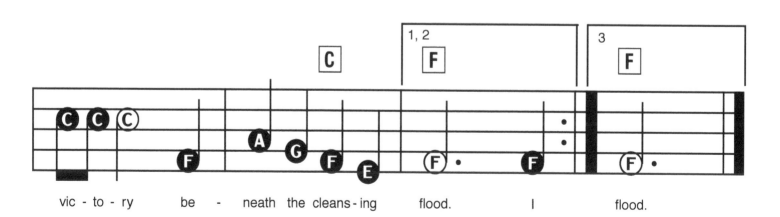

vic - to - ry be - neath the cleans - ing flood. I flood.

Wings of a Dove

Registration 2
Rhythm: Waltz

Words and Music by
Bob Ferguson

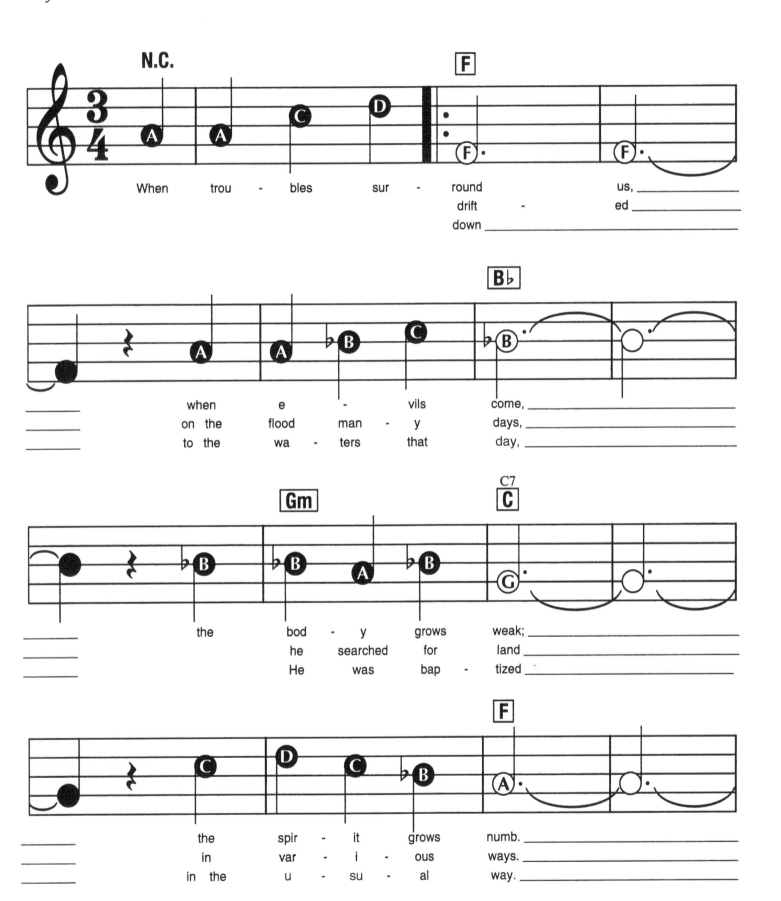

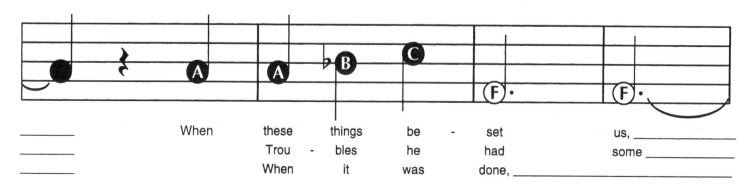

When these things be - set us, _____
Trou - bles he had some _____
When it was done, _____

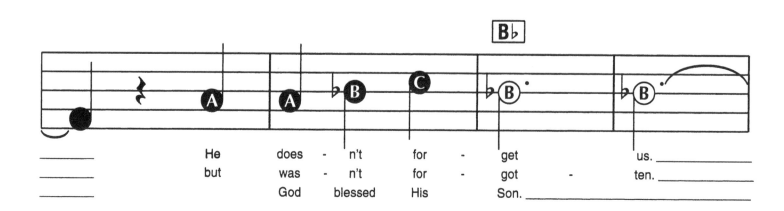

He does - n't for - get us. _____
but was - n't for - got - ten. _____
God blessed His Son. _____

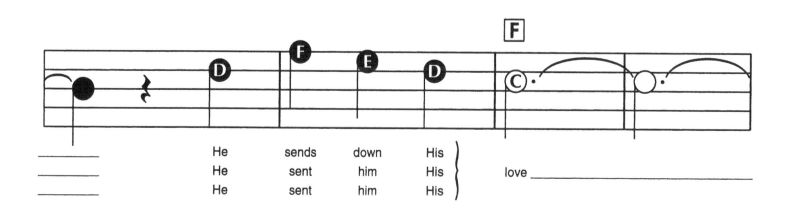

He sends down His ⎫
He sent him His ⎬ love _____
He sent him His ⎭

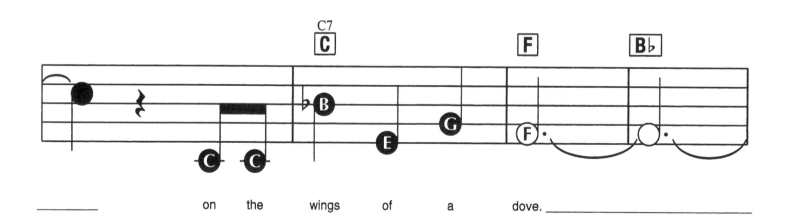

on the wings of a dove. _____

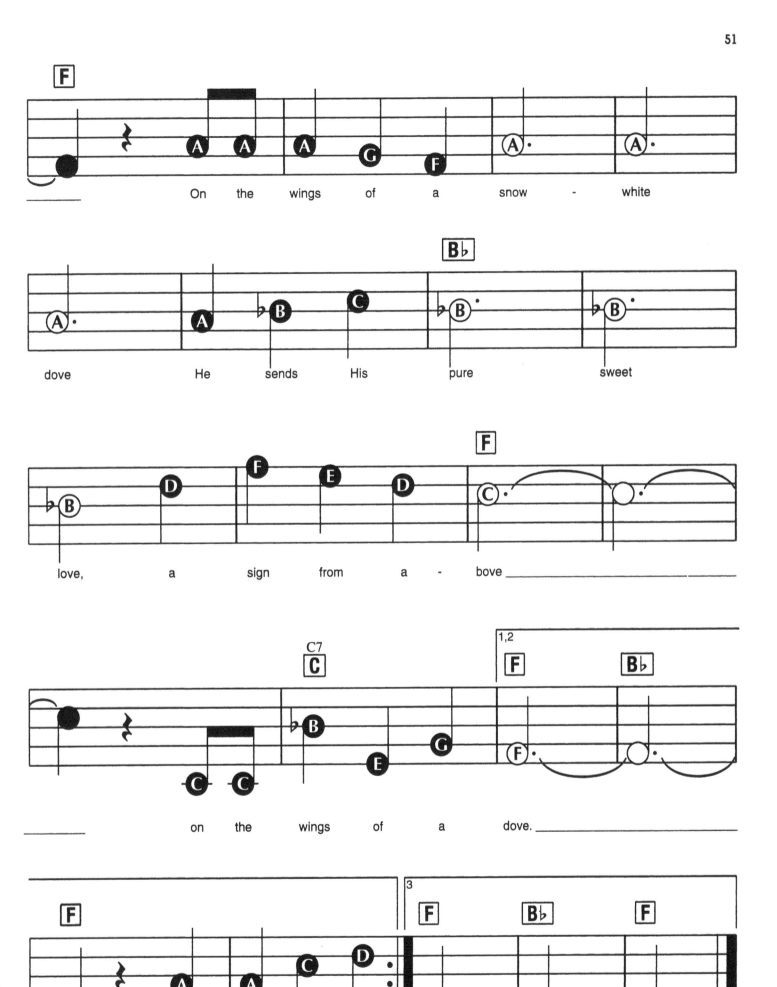

A Wonderful Time Up There
(Everybody's Gonna Have a Wonderful Time Up There)

Registration 4
Rhythm: Fox Trot or Country

Words and Music by
Lee Roy Abernathy

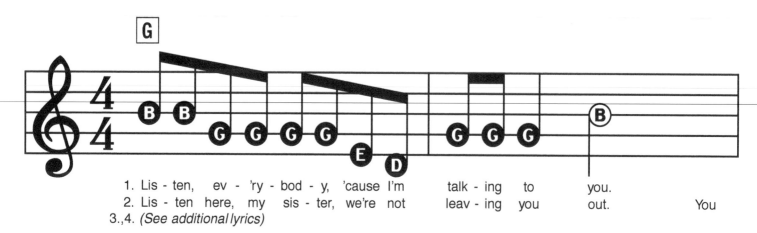

1. Lis - ten, ev - 'ry - bod - y, 'cause I'm talk - ing to you.
2. Lis - ten here, my sis - ter, we're not leav - ing you out. You
3.,4. *(See additional lyrics)*

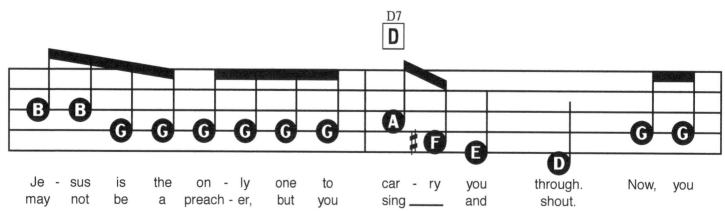

Je - sus is the on - ly one to car - ry you through. Now, you
may not be a preach - er, but you sing ____ and shout.

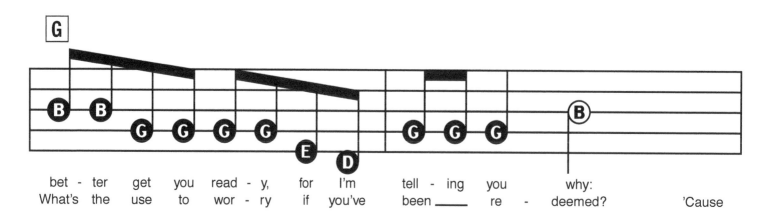

bet - ter get you read - y, for I'm tell - ing you why:
What's the use to wor - ry if you've been ____ re - deemed? 'Cause

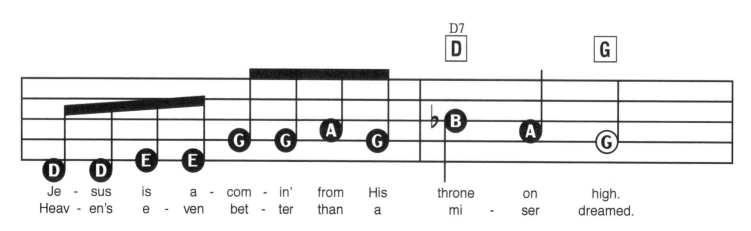

Je - sus is a - com - in' from His throne on high.
Heav - en's e - ven bet - ter than a mi - ser dreamed.

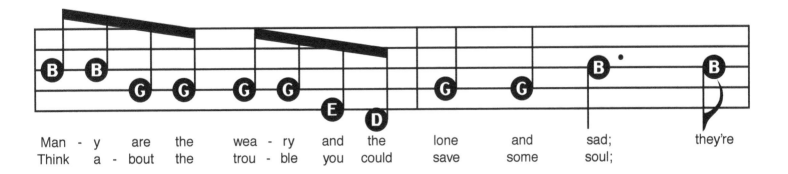

Man - y are the wea - ry and the lone and sad; they're
Think a - bout the trou - ble you could save some soul;

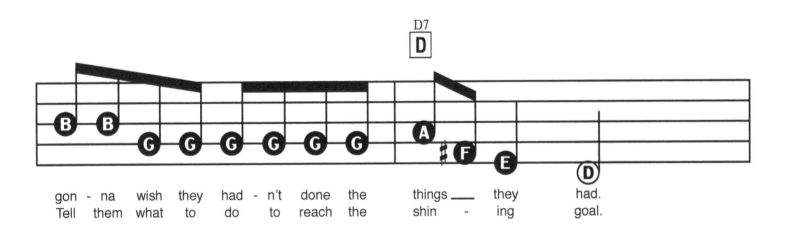

gon - na wish they had - n't done the things ___ they had.
Tell them what to do to reach the shin - ing goal.

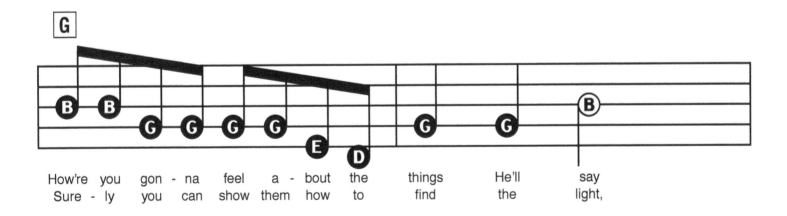

How're you gon - na feel a - bout the things He'll say
Sure - ly you can show them how to find the light,

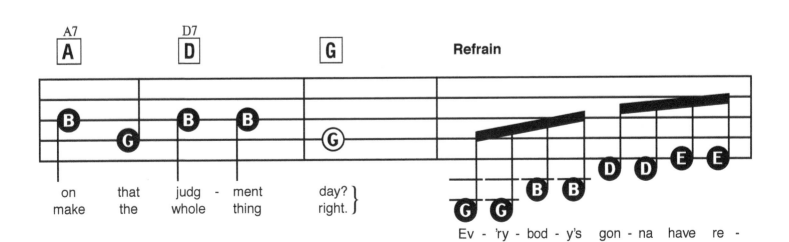

on that judg - ment day?
make the whole thing right.

Ev - 'ry - bod - y's gon - na have re -

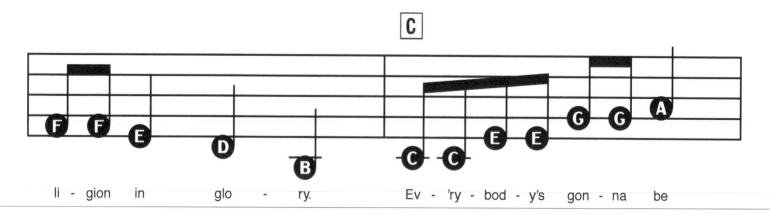

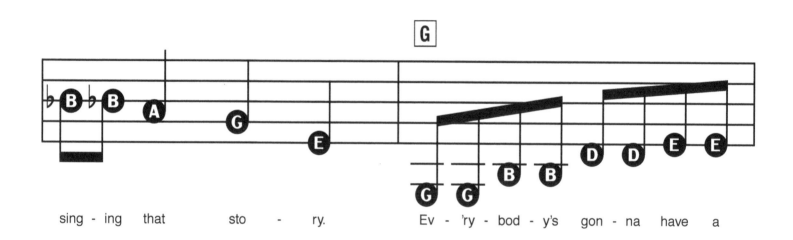

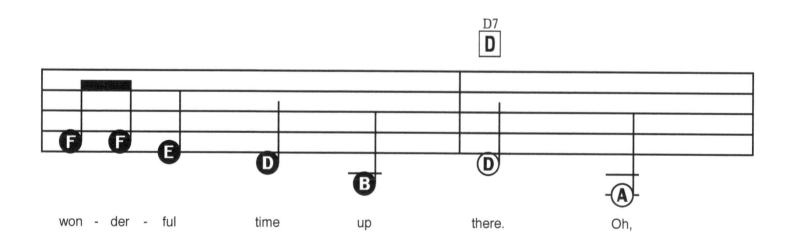

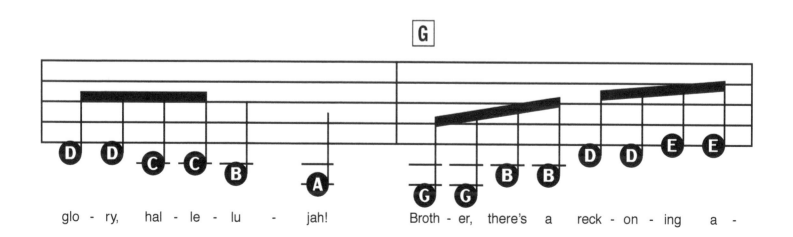

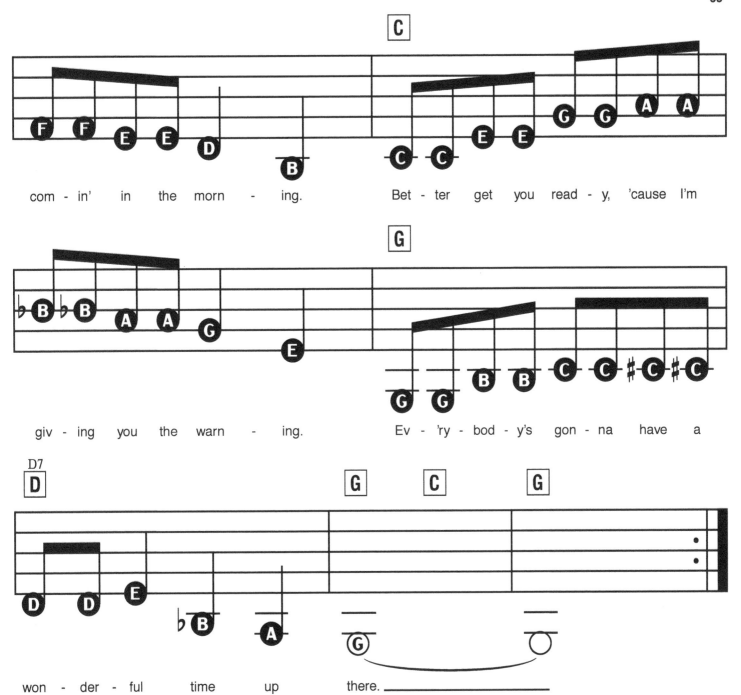

com - in' in the morn - ing. Bet - ter get you read - y, 'cause I'm

giv - ing you the warn - ing. Ev - 'ry - bod - y's gon - na have a

won - der - ful time up there. _____

Additional Lyrics

3. When the tribulations seem to darken the way,
   That's the time to get down on your knees and pray.
   Ev'rybody's gonna have their troubles, too;
   Gotta be so careful 'bout the things we do.
   We're going down the valley, going one by one,
   Gonna be rewarded for the things we've done.
   When we get to Heaven and the Promised Land,
   Then we'll understand.
   Refrain

4. Now get your Holy Bible in the back of the book.
   The book of Revelation, that's the place you must look.
   If you understand it, and you can if you try,
   Jesus is a-comin' from His throne on high.
   Reading in the Bible all the things that He said,
   Said He was a-comin' back to raise the dead.
   Are you gonna be among the chosen few?
   Will you make it through?
   Refrain

FOR ORGANS, PIANOS & ELECTRONIC KEYBOARDS

E-Z PLAY® TODAY PUBLICATIONS

The E-Z Play® Today songbook series is the shortest distance between beginning music and playing fun!
Check out this list of highlights and visit balleonard.com for a complete listing of all volumes and songlists.

HAL•LEONARD®

Prices, contents and availability subject to change without notice

0421
330